Amazing
Guitar
Facts and Trivia

Amazing Guitar
Facts and Trivia

NIGEL CAWTHORNE

CHARTWELL
BOOKS, INC.

A QUARTO BOOK

Published in 2011 by
Chartwell Books, Inc.
A division of Book Sales, Inc.
276 Fifth Avenue, Suite 206
New York, New York 10001
USA

Copyright © 2011 Quarto Inc.

ISBN 978-0-7858-2834-1

Conceived, designed,
and produced by
Quarto Publishing plc
The Old Brewery
6 Blundell Street
London N7 9BH

QUA: AGFT

Design: Schermuly Design Co.
Editor: Cathy Meeus
Proofreader: Lynn Bresler
Indexer: Richard Emerson
Art director: Caroline Guest

Creative director: Moira Clinch
Publisher: Paul Carslake

Color separation by Modern Age
Repro House Ltd, Hong Kong
Printed by Midas Printing
International Ltd, China

CONTENTS

The contents of this book are
completely random, so that each time
you open it, you will discover an
amazing variety of facts and trivia
about the guitar. If you wish to locate a particular category
of information however, this contents list is organized into
topics. There is also an index on pages 186–192.

DESIGN AND DETAILS

GUITAR MATERIALS

PERSONALITIES

INTRODUCTION

With the birth of rock 'n' roll in the 1950s, the electric guitar took over as the leading solo instrument in a band from the brass instruments that had ruled jazz.

Before, the acoustic guitar had been just too quiet to make an impact. Then as the power of electrical amplification grew, the guitar blew every other instrument off the stage.

The guitar had done this once before. In the 16th century, played by strolling troubadours and in court, it had taken over from the lute because it was easier to play. It was a democratic instrument played by both monarchs and their minions. It has also always been a sexy instrument, used by swains to woo their damsels.

Although in the 18th and 19th centuries guitarists had toured Europe, playing to packed concert halls, it was largely eclipsed by the social cachet of orchestral music. It was in the United States that it came into its own. The cheap, portable guitar could be used to accompany the folk songs sung by cowboys and hillbillies and the gritty

ditties of traveling bluesmen. You did not even have to go to a music store to buy one. They were readily available mail order.

With the rise of rap and hip-hop, many predict that the 50-year reign of guitar bands is over, but across the world young hopefuls are still disappearing into the garage with their "ax" in the sure and certain knowledge that they are going to be the next big thing.

Amazing Guitar Facts and Trivia is an instant introduction to the history and the world of fascinating anecdotes related to this instrument, reflecting the fun it is to listen to, study, and play. Somewhere within all of us—even if it is only with an air guitar in front of the bedroom mirror—there lurks a guitar hero trying to get out.

RESONATING SUCCESS

Also known as the resophonic guitar or Dobro, the resonator guitar was developed by the Slovak-born inventors John and Rudy Dopyera in 1925 after John was approached by Texan steel-guitar player George Beauchamp, who wanted a guitar loud enough to be heard over an orchestra. John Dopyera came up with a design based on that of the Stroh violin, in which the vibrations of the strings passed through the bridge to a small, sensitive disk and were then amplified through a horn. But the Dopyeras used metal cones to amplify the sound. They experimented with a number of materials before settling on aluminum, which had only become widely available in the 1890s.

Weber Bandit resophonic guitar

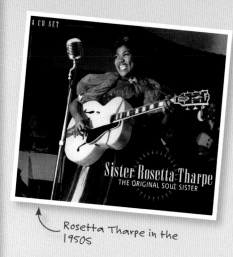

Rosetta Tharpe in the 1950s

The godmother of rock 'n' roll

The first great exponent of the electric guitar was gospel-singer Sister Rosetta Tharpe. Born Rosetta Nubin in Cotton Plant, Arkansas, in 1915, she sang and played the guitar from the age of six alongside her mother, the evangelist Katie Bell Nubin, at revival meetings.

When the family moved to Chicago in the 1920s, she continued her public career in gospel, while playing blues and jazz in private. She learned to "bend" the note on her guitar in imitation of jazz musicians. Beginning her recording career in 1938, by the 1950s she had moved from the acoustic to the electric guitar, playing a Gibson Les Paul. She toured with Muddy Waters and inspired Elvis Presley, Little Richard, Jerry Lee Lewis, Johnny Cash, Chuck Berry, and Bob Dylan. Touring the U.K. in 1964 she also influenced a new generation of British guitarists. Rosetta Tharpe was the pioneer of the use of distortion, later attributed to Eric Clapton and Jimi Hendrix. She died in 1973 and in 2007 was inducted posthumously into the Blues Hall of Fame.

Ana Moura playing a Portuguese 12-string at Festival Med, in Loule, Portugal, 2008.

THE PORTUGUESE 12-STRING

In the 19th century the Portuguese introduced the 12-string guitar. Early in the 20th century two discrete models became standard—the Coimbra with a free string length of 18½ inches (47 cm) from the Coimbra region and the shorter Lisboa with a free string length of 17½ inches (44.5 cm) from Lisbon. The Lisboa has a larger sounding board, a narrower neck, and an ornamental scroll adorning the tuning machine.

Traditionally the Portuguese 12-string guitar is played employing a technique called *dediho*, using only the thumb and index finger. The other fingers rest on the sounding board and pluck the strings with the corner of the fingernails.

The first fanzine

Beethoven is known to have attended the concerts of the Italian guitarist Mauro Giuliani (1781–1829). Giuliani was appointed to the court of the Empress Marie-Louise, Napoleon's wife. In an attempt to satisfy his public Giuliani wrote over a hundred works for the guitar. In England, enthusiasts started a magazine devoted to him called *The Giulianiad*, which argued that the guitar was the equal of, if not superior to, the piano.

MARTIN MODEL CODING

Martin guitars have a simple code. A *letter* denoting the size is followed by a hyphen, then a number specifying the style.

Size

O	Concert size
OO	Grand concert size
OOO	Auditorium size
D	Dreadnought size
DS	Dreadnought with 12 frets to the body
M	Grand auditorium size
MC	Grand auditorium size with cutaway body
OM	Orchestral model
C	Classical
N	Classical (European)
F	F-hole model

Style

16	Spruce top, quarter sawn mahogany back and sides, wide rosewood fingerboard, no fret markers or fingerplate, and a slotted headstock
18	Solid headstock, "belly" bridge, 14 frets to the body, white dot position markers, dark fingerplate and edgings
28	Spruce soundboard with white edging, rosewood back and sides
45	Spruce top, rosewood back and sides, ebony fingerboard, and abalone pearl inlays

The classic Martin D-45 has a Dreadnought body with a spruce top, rosewood back and sides, ebony fingerboard, and abalone pearl inlays.

The head of a headless guitar

The headless guitar

Ned Steinberger is the originator of the headless guitar. In his designs the neck does not end in a tuning machine. Rather it is squared off. Micrometer-style tuners are found in the tailpiece. His guitars need strings with balls at both ends.

His most famous design is the L-series, which is shaped like a flattened besom broom or an oar. The body is made from carbon fiber and graphite. This makes the guitar extremely light and gives it a clean sound, which some see as a bad thing. Making a virtue out of necessity, Steinberger coined the slogan: "We don't make 'em like they used to."

He went on to make many more headless guitar designs, including the P-series with an A-shaped wooden body and a bolt-on composite neck. His G-series had a headstock—but it featured his own design of 40:1 gearless tuners.

GIBSON LES PAUL STANDARD

1958

In 1952, with Fender Telecaster sales taking off, Gibson contacted Les Paul—the "funny guy with the broomstick," who had tried to interest them in a solid-body guitar years before. They came up with the Les Paul Goldtop with a maple cap stuck to a thick, mahogany bass. The front was carved and finished in metallic gold. Although it sold well, people were getting used to the modern look and sound of the Fenders. So in 1958 Gibson ditched the gold and sprayed the body with a cherry-red sunburst, the classic Standard look. But neither could this model compete with the Fenders and went out of production in 1960 after just 1,700 had been made. Six years later, a young Eric Clapton swapped his Telecaster for a Les Paul Standard. Soon they were changing hands in London for £400 ($600) and in 1968 the Les Paul Standard went back into production.

This Gibson Les Paul is Jimmy Page's "Number one."

22 frets

Rosewood fingerboards

Mahogany neck

Pearloid "crown" position markers

Three-way pickup selector

Cherry sunburst finish (over the years other colors have been offered, including black, red, and tobacco sunburst)

Two humbucker pickups

Top edge bound in cream plastic

Solid mahogany body with book-matched, two-piece flame maple cap

Twin volume and tone controls

Pearloid "crown" position markers

Famous players

☆ Eric Clapton
☆ Jimmy Page
☆ Peter Green
☆ Jeff Beck
☆ Duane Allman
☆ Mike Bloomfield
☆ Noel Gallagher of Oasis
☆ Neil Young
☆ Paul Kossoff
☆ Gary Moore
Al Di Meola
☆ Slash of Guns N' Roses
☆ Joe Walsh and Don Felder of The Eagles
☆ Billy Gibbons of ZZ Top
☆ Scott Gorham of Thin Lizzy

The world's smallest guitar

Researchers at Cornell University's Nanotechnology Center have made a guitar that is one ten-millionth of a meter in length. That's one-twentieth of the width of a human hair. Based on the design of a Fender Stratocaster, it could fit inside a red blood cell. The strings have a width of about fifty-billionths of a meter, just 100 atoms wide. Plucked by a laser plectrum, they produce an inaudible pitch of around 10 megahertz—130,000 times or 17 octaves higher than a normal guitar. The egg heads at Cornell explain: "We're trying to figure out what sort of new possibilities are allowed by this optical method of interacting with mechanical devices."

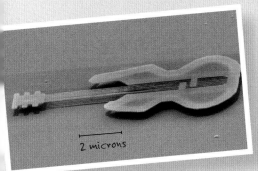

2 microns

CIGAR-BOX GUITARS

African-Americans who were taken to the United States as slaves brought no possessions with them. But they had not lost their love of music and made primitive stringed instruments using a gourd called a "banjar," which evolved into the banjo. Later they made square guitars from a cigar box with a plank of wood nailed to it to make a neck. These were made from the 1840s onwards. Until then cigars had been shipped in large crates that contained over a hundred cigars. Later they were packed in small boxes of twenties or fifties that were a more suitable size to be made into an instrument. One made in around 1861 is on display in the Smithsonian Museum, Washington, D.C.

Following the end of the Civil War, with slaves leaving the plantations and soldiers returning home, cigar-box guitars spread across the country. The legendary blues guitarist Charlie Christian had one, B.B.

A collection of antique cigar-box guitars, banjos, and ukuleles from the National Cigar Box Guitar Museum

King's father made King one when he could not afford the $2 for a store-bought guitar, while Lightin' Hopkins made his own. "I got me a cigar box," he said. "I cut me a round hole in the middle of it, take me a little piece of plank, nailed it onto that cigar box, and I got me some screen wire and I made me a bridge back there and raised it up high enough that it would sound inside that little box."

Has that mean guitar player gone yet?

Although the strings of an acoustic guitar were traditionally referred to as "cat gut," they were usually made out of dried sheep's intestines.

ALL STRUNG OUT

Towards the end of the 19th century steel began to supersede gut as the most common material for guitar strings, and by the 1920s they had taken over completely. On a standard guitar, only the top two or three strings are made from a single strand of steel. The remainder are "wrapped" strings where the inner core has a second strand of wire wound tightly around it. This makes the strings easier to play and affects the sound.

There are three types of winding:
- **Roundwound strings** use a conventional wire with a circular section wound around the core. These are the most common on both electric and acoustic guitars, and give a bright treble sound.
- **Flatwound strings** have a flat ribbon of steel wound round the inner core. These are often used on arch-top guitars, giving a smoother feel but a less bright tone. The advantage is they cut down the sound of the fingers on the strings. Their disadvantage is that they break easily.
- **Groundwound strings** attempt to combine the advantages of the other two types. They are essentially roundwound strings that are then ground to flatten them.

Tie it down

To cut down feedback, Les Paul made one of his early guitars out of a railroad tie.

The Martin headstock

Copying the classical designs he made for Johann Stauffer back in Vienna, C.F. Martin originally placed all the tuning pegs on one side of the headstock. Although the company abandoned that feature after Martin died in 1873, the idea was revived by later guitar makers such as Paul Bigsby and Leo Fender.

TIRED OF STEEL

In the 1940s early rock-'n'-rollers such as Ike Turner used to burn car tires to get steel cord to string their guitars.

Traditional "Open Coil" (uncovered) humbucker pickup

THE HUMBUCKER

The "humbucking coil" was invented in 1934 by the audio company Electro-Voice of South Bend, Indiana, as a means of reducing the hum generated by the amplifier. Then in 1955 Seth Lover at Gibson came up with a new version that was used on the Gibson Les Paul. Also known as the humberbucker or humbucking pickup, the 1955 humbucker uses two coils with opposing windings and polarities. They reinforce the signal induced by the vibrating metal guitar string, while canceling out the electrical hum picked up from the electricity supply.

100 Greatest Guitarists of All Time

Rolling Stone magazine has listed the 100 Greatest Guitarists of All Time. They were:

1 Jimi Hendrix
2 Duane Allman
3 B.B. King
4 Eric Clapton
5 Robert Johnson
6 Chuck Berry
7 Stevie Ray Vaughan
8 Ry Cooder
9 Jimmy Page
10 Keith Richards
11 Kirk Hammett
12 Kurt Cobain
13 Jerry Garcia
14 Jeff Beck
15 Carlos Santana
16 Johnny Ramone
17 Jack White
18 John Frusciante
19 Richard Thompson
20 James Burton
21 George Harrison
22 Mike Bloomfield
23 Warren Haynes
24 The Edge
25 Freddy King
26 Tom Morello
27 Mark Knopfler
28 Stephen Stills
29 Ron Asheton
30 Buddy Guy
31 Rick Dale
32 John Cipollina
33 Lee Ranaldo
34 Thurston Moore

Continued on p.22

FENDER STRATOCASTER

1954

The Stratocaster is the ultimate guitar hero icon, as recognizable as a Coca-Cola bottle or a Volkswagen Beetle. It provided the piercing treble pickup sound of Buddy Holly's "Peggy Sue," the warm neck tone of Jimi Hendrix's "The Wind Cries Mary," and the hollow, wiry voice of Dire Straits' "Sultans of Swing." The Stratocaster was produced in response to criticism of Fender's earlier Telecaster, which had sharp edges, was uncomfortable to hold, and just too plain. Fender's answer was the sleek, two-horned Stratocaster. Designed by Freddie Tavares and honed in extensive field tests by country guitarist Bill Carson, its smoothly contoured body featured a double cutaway to make it easy to reach the high notes. The molded contours and the rounded edges made it comfortable to play. The Strat had three pickups for unmatched tonal variation. The stagger pickup was aimed to give even volume across all six strings, but musicians soon found that you could jam the three-way switch control in an intermediate position to produce a unique "out of phase" sound.

2007 Fender American VG Stratocaster

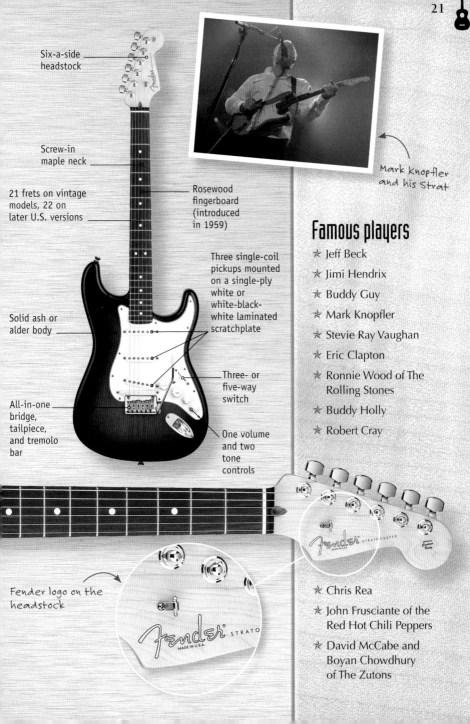

Six-a-side headstock

Screw-in maple neck

21 frets on vintage models, 22 on later U.S. versions

Rosewood fingerboard (introduced in 1959)

Three single-coil pickups mounted on a single-ply white or white-black-white laminated scratchplate

Solid ash or alder body

Three- or five-way switch

All-in-one bridge, tailpiece, and tremolo bar

One volume and two tone controls

Mark Knopfler and his Strat

Famous players

* Jeff Beck
* Jimi Hendrix
* Buddy Guy
* Mark Knopfler
* Stevie Ray Vaughan
* Eric Clapton
* Ronnie Wood of The Rolling Stones
* Buddy Holly
* Robert Cray

Fender logo on the headstock

* Chris Rea
* John Frusciante of the Red Hot Chili Peppers
* David McCabe and Boyan Chowdhury of The Zutons

100 Greatest Guitarists of All Time, continued from p.19

Continued on p.23

PAPER GUITAR

Spanish guitar maker Antonio de Torres (1817–92) built a guitar with its back and sides made out of papier-mâché. It can now be seen at the Museu de la Música in Barcelona.

Picks made from Gibeon meteorites

Pick of the bunch

Rick Nielsen of Cheap Trick used to throw guitar picks out into the audience. But he would not do it with picks made by the Australian company Starpics. They are fashioned from precious materials. The most expensive fetch over $4,000 and are made from Gibeon meteorites found in the Namibian desert in Africa in 1836. The meteorites are thought to be around four billion years old. Export of the meteorites has been banned, but over 25 tons of them have found their way out of the country.

> **Jimmy Page is definitely one of the great guitarists. And he has the great advantage of still being alive.**
>
> SLASH OF GUNS N' ROSES

TINY TWANGER

The retailer Hammacher Schlemmer has produced the world's smallest fully functional electric guitar. At just 26½ inches (67 cm) long, 6 inches (15 cm) wide, and 1½ inches (4 cm) deep, it's smaller than the neck of any normal electric guitar, the manufacturers say. With a humbucker pickup and a 20-fret neck, it "retains the punch and kick, as well as the precision of any Ibanez or Jackson."

Bonnie Guitar

The wife of electric-guitar pioneer Paul Tutmarc, Bonnie (née Buckingham), became a country singer under the name Bonnie Guitar and had a hit in 1957 with "Dark Moon."

Continued from p.22

75 Adam Jones
76 Ali Farka Touré
77 Henry Vestine
78 Robbie Robertson
79 Cliff Gallup
80 Robert Quine
81 Derek Trucks
82 David Gilmour
83 Neil Young
84 Eddie Cochran
85 Randy Rhoads
86 Tommy Iommi
87 Joan Jett
88 Dave Davies
89 D. Boon
90 Glen Buxton
91 Robby Krieger
92 Wayne Kramer
93 Fred "Sonic" Smith
94 Bert Jansch
95 Kevin Shields
96 Angus Young
97 Robert Randolph
98 Leigh Stephens
99 Greg Ginn
100 Kim Thayil

THE SEVEN-STRING GUITAR

While the six-string guitar and its 12-string variant have been the norm for around 200 years, in 1964 jazz guitarist George Van Eps had a seven-string model made by Brooklyn guitar manufacturer Gretsch from experimental designs he had developed with Epiphone 20 years early. The seventh string was tuned to B, giving the guitar a range of four-and-a-half octaves.

Although the idea failed to catch on generally, Steve Vai of the band Whitesnake collaborated with Ibanez Guitars to make a seven-stringed Universe guitar in the late 1980s. Modern jazzmen Howard Alden and Steve Masakowski also use seven-string models. Masakowski's guitar, custom made for him by New Orleans maker Sal Giardina, has the extra string tuned to A, five extra frets to extend the range, and a headless neck.

Ibanez seven-string Universe guitar

MAIL ORDER
In 1927 you could buy a guitar from the Sears Roebuck catalog for as little as $4.95.

Musicians on an Ancient Greek urn

Guitars of the ancient world

Carvings of guitar-like instruments dating from at least 5,000 years ago have been found in Susa, the ancient capital of Persia (modern-day Iran). In ancient Egypt they had a guitar-like long-necked lute. In classical Greece, this was called a kithara, which may have lent its name to the modern instrument.

Back view of a modern
chitarra battente

CHITARRA BATTENTE

In the 17th century the five-string chitarra battente—or "beating guitar"—came into fashion. It had wire strings and was played with a plectrum. The frets were made from a hard material and the top was slightly arched to increase the tension on the strings as they passed over the bridge. The back was also arched in most guitars of that period.

A modern chitarra battente made by Italian luthier Antonio Dattis

SET-UPS OF THE STARS

Pete Townshend

In the early days of The Who, Pete Townshend played an Emile Grimshaw SS Deluxe, plus six- and 12-string Rickenbackers. From the late 1960s, he favored a Gretsch in the studio and a Gibson for live work. Since the 1980s, he has preferred the Fender Eric Clapton Stratocaster to his own signature model.

GIBSON FLYING V

1958

To keep up with Fender, Gibson needed something that looked modern. Legend has it that the designers came up with a hundred or so candidates. The list was whittled down to just three—the Moderne, the Flying V, and the Firebird. But the Flying V proved too radical. It was ridiculed on its release, shipped only 98 in the first year, and rapidly went out of production. However, it re-emerged in 1967. Two found their way into the hands of Jimi Hendrix—one standard issue, which Hendrix painted in psychedelic colors, and a black one, custom made for him by Gibson. Its success was assured when Jimi Hendrix played it on "All Along the Watchtower" and "Voodoo Chile (Slight Return)."

Black bobbin humbucker pickup

1958 Gibson Flying V

Rosewood
fingerboard

Pearloid dots

Lenny
Kravitz with
his Gibson
Flying V on
the cover
of his album
Baptism

Glued-in
neck

Twin humbuckers
(later versions
have pickups
mounted on a
large scratchplate)

Clear cellulose
finish

Solid two-piece
korina wood
body (later
versions have a
mahogany body)

Ridged rubber
strip along
lower edge to
prevent slipping
when playing
sitting down

Dual volume
and master
tone control

Famous players

* ✷ Jimi Hendrix
* ✷ Dave Davies
  of The Kinks
* ✷ Lonnie Mack
* ✷ Rick Derringer
* ✷ Albert King
* ✷ Johnny Winter
* ✷ Andy Powell of
  Wishbone Ash
* ✷ Billy Gibbons
* ✷ Marc Bolan
* ✷ Lenny Kravitz

The Gibson Flying V was a
commercial failure when first
launched. Today, early models
fetch over $50,000.

THE APPLICATION OF SCIENCE

In the 1960s the physical chemist Dr. Michael Kasha bought a classical guitar for his son and, although Kasha was not a musician, he felt that the application of science might make it sound better. In a 30-year collaboration with luthier Richard Schneider he aimed to turn up to 8 percent of the energy in the strings into sound (compared with only 5 percent in traditional classical guitars). Together they concentrated on five areas:

1 The neck was made rigid and heavy to prevent energy from the string being lost in vibration to increase the treble response.

2 The bridge was shaped like a wedge to carry the treble tones to the right half of the soundboard and the bass tones to the left. It was also lightened to increase response.

3 The soundboard was made thinner in the bass half and thicker in the treble half to make it more responsive to those tones. The sound hole was moved from the centerline, creating a larger vibrating area. This also allowed the interior braces to be the appropriate length for the midrange.

4 The entire bracing system was rearranged to reinforce the production of treble tones by the treble half of the top and bass tones by the bass half. It also allowed the bridge to move more freely, adding richer harmonics and more sustain.

5 The back had a complex bracing system that allowed it to move like the diaphragm of a speaker.

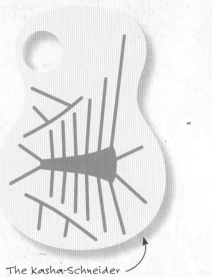

The Kasha-Schneider bracing system with hole moved from the center

THE SHARK

Eddie Van Halen had a guitar called the "Shark." It was an Ibanez Destroyer out of which Eddie cut large chunks of wood with a hacksaw. The resulting shape looked like sharks' teeth. The mutilated guitar can be seen on the videos of "You Really Got Me" and "Runnin' With The Devil." Unfortunately, this radical surgery ruined the sound of the guitar, and Eddie was unable to to get a replacement.

Blind Boy Fuller

Born in Wadesboro, North Carolina, in 1908, Fulton Allen gradually lost his sight, becoming completely blind at the age of 20. He took to the streets with his guitar under the name "Blind Boy Fuller." He became an ace fingerpicker and leading exponent of the East Coast Piedmont style of guitar playing shared by Gary Davis and Blind Blake. He moved to the tobacco town of Winston-Salem, then to Durham, where he played to the workers as they left the factory. In a brief recording career from 1935 to 1940, he recorded 150 songs, but died tragically young of kidney disease in 1941.

KNOW YOUR GAUGE
Strings come in different gauges. Lighter strings are easier to hold down and bend, while heavier strings produce greater volume and sustain.

On the Air with FRED WARING FIVE NITES A WEEK, MON. THRU FRI. OVER N-B-C

LES PAUL
Sensation of the ELECTRIC GUITAR who does the un-usual and the unexpected on his *Gibson* ES-300

ONLY A *Gibson* IS GOOD ENOUGH

Gibson, INC., KALAMAZOO, MICH.
WRITE FOR CATALOGUES

LES PAUL FACTS

✪ He nearly electrocuted himself while undertaking early experiments with electric guitars.

✪ In 1948 he had a near-fatal automobile accident that destroyed the tendons in his elbow. He opted to have it fixed at a 90-degree angle so he could still play a guitar.

✪ He pioneered the art of multi-tracking.

✪ He coined the idea of the headless bass.

✪ In his 80s he claimed to be working on a new design of guitar "that would blow everybody away."

GATHERING MOSS
Rolling Stones' guitarist keith Richards has a collection of over a thousand guitars.

A National Triolian finished in yellow and walnut brown sunburst

Changing colors

When the Triolian went into production in 1929 it was finished in Polychrome paint—an unusual yellow with red and blue highlights—and floral decal patterns, or pictures of anemones, hula girls, and palm trees. The following year the Triolian was given a steel body and was finished in green-tinted Polychrome or in a yellow and walnut brown sunburst. Then from 1937 to 1941, it was painted to simulate rosewood.

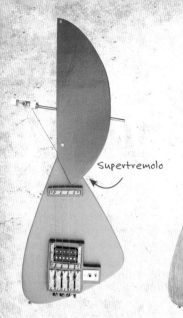

Supertremolo

Blonde
stereo guitar

Overtone
zither

GUITARLAND, MAN

Dutch comic-book artist and experimental luthier Yuri Landman specializes in making weird and wonderful guitars and other eccentric stringed instruments. Between 2000 and 2005, he built

✪ A four-string, blue supertremolo guitar with an adjustable pitch control for the left hand instead of a fretboard.

✪ The Robocop, a six-string, heavily adjusted guitar with two additional bridges and three outputs.

✪ A three-string, blonde stereo guitar with one bass string and two thin guitar strings all tuned to B.

✪ A seven-string, green trio-guitar, one bass string, three guitar strings tuned DAD, and three G# strings.

✪ A four-string black zither with a movable third bridge.

✪ A red "capozither," as shown on the cover of *Vivre dans l'aisance*, a CD by Landman's band Avec Aisance.

✪ A 12-string overtone zither, the prototype of the guitar-shaped Moodswinger zither.

✪ The electric cymbalum with 72 strings and 12 pickups.

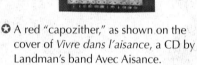

Washburn guitars

The Washburn guitar company was started in Chicago in 1883. In the 1920s their instruments became the guitar of choice for bluesmen coming from the South, who played on nearby Maxwell Street.

GRETSCH WHITE FALCON

1955

When the White Falcon was unveiled at the National Association of Music Merchants show in July 1954, it was billed at the "dream guitar" and the "guitar of the future." But it was just a showpiece. Gretsch had no plans to put it into production. However, the sheer volume of interest changed their minds. The White Falcon cost $600—at a time when you could buy a family car for $1,000.

Nevertheless, it was an instant success. But over the years, Gretsch attempted to improve it. By the late 1960s, it was covered in controls and knobs, making it almost unplayable. The new generation of guitarist favored Stratocasters and Les Pauls. However, in the 1970s it resurfaced as a favored guitar of Crosby, Stills, Nash & Young and has continued to appeal to succeeding generations of players.

1955 Gretsch White Falcon

Gold sparkle headstock with inlaid "wings"

Ebony fingerboard

Glued-in maple neck

Single cutaway (changed to a double cutaway in the early 1960s)

All-white finish

Master volume control

Three-way switch

Gold sparkle binding

Gold pickguard with painted falcon

Twin pickups

Tone control

Cadillac "G" tailpiece (though Bigsby available)

Two volume controls

AC/DC pin

Wing motifs etched into the inlays

Famous players

- ☆ Stephen Stills
- ☆ Neil Young
- ☆ David Crosby
- ☆ John Frusciante of the Red Hot Chili Peppers
- ☆ Billy Duffy of The Cult
- ☆ Brian Setzer of Stray Cats
- ☆ Malcolm Young of AC/DC

THE FENDER GRUNGEMASTER

Jazz guitarists are old fashioned. They want big, hollow-body guitars with traditional looks and fat-sounding humbuckers. In 1958 Leo Fender came up with the Jazzmaster that did not give them any of those things— and it cost $50 more than a Stratocaster. They shunned it. However, two decades later it became the darling of punk, new wave, indie, garage, and grunge bands. Those who have used it include Elvis Costello, Tom Verlaine, the Ventures, Thurston Moore of Sonic Youth, Thom Yorke of Radiohead, and J. Mascis of the Dinosaur Jr.

66 I never liked mellow-sounding guitars. I bought a Fender Jazzmaster in New York, which in those days was $95 because nobody wanted 'em. Now they're up to $400, probably because Elvis Costello had his picture taken with 'em so many times. 99

TOM VERLAINE

Elvis Costello playing a Fender Jazzmaster guitar

Pete Townshend smashes his guitar against an amplifier on stage.

TOWNSHEND VERSUS HENDRIX

When Jimi Hendrix arrived in London in 1966, Pete Townshend feared his guitar-smashing days were over. "Hendrix was the first man to walk all over my territory," said Townshend. "I felt incredibly intimidated by that." While Townshend merely played his guitar in the conventional style, then smashed it to pieces, Hendrix played his behind the back of his neck, with his teeth, then set fire to it.

SET-UPS OF THE STARS

The Edge

The lead guitar of U2 plays a Stratocaster or Gibson Explorer given multiple rhythmic delays by an Electro-Harmonix Deluxe Memory Man. He has added a range of analog and digital effects. The resultant sound signal is routed to a number of Vox AC30s.

> *There's a difficulty in finding reasonably priced, high-quality lefthand guitars.*
>
> KURT COBAIN

THE WORLD'S TEN MOST EXPENSIVE GUITARS

1. $2.7 million. *"Reach out to Asia" Fender Stratocaster*
A Fender Stratocaster became officially the most expensive guitar in the world when it sold at auction in Qatar on November 16, 2005, to raise funds for "Reach out to Asia," a charity formed to help the tsunami victims. For the charity auction, organized by Bryan Adams, the guitar had been signed by Mick Jagger, Keith Richards, Eric Clapton, Brian May, Jimmy Page, David Gilmour, Jeff Beck, Pete Townshend, Mark Knopfler, Ray Davis, Liam Gallagher, Ronnie Wood, Tony Iommi, Angus and Malcolm Young, Paul McCartney, Sting, Ritchie Blackmore, Def Leppard, and Bryan Adams himself. The Strat had been bought for $1 million the year before by the Qatari royal family, who then donated the money to the charity. Then it was sold again at the auction for $2.7 million, raising a total of $3.7 million dollars.

Continued on p.37

Classic woods

The following are the woods most commonly used in making classical guitars:

- Alpine spruce from Switzerland and Germany
- Sitka spruce from North America
- Western red cedar
- Indian rosewood
- Brazilian rosewood
- Maple
- Pear wood
- Honduras cedar
- Mahogany
- Ebony
- Spanish cypress

Mahogany

Maple

Western red cedar

Indian rosewood

Ebony

> **July 27, 1661—To Westminster, where at Mr. Montagu's chamber I heard a Frenchman play, a friend of Monsieur Eschar's, upon the guitar, most extreme well, though at the best methinks it is but a bawble.**

SAMUEL PEPYS

Antonio de Torres

Spanish guitarist and carpenter Antonio de Torres (1817–92) fixed the shape of the classical acoustic guitar. Working with the guitarist and composer Julián Arcas (1832–82), he made guitars louder by making them larger and using a thinner, lighter soundboard that was arched in both directions. To maintain the strength of the structure, he added bracing struts.

An 1858 classical guitar by Antonio de Torres

Continued from p.36

2. $2 million (estimated value) *Jimi Hendrix's 1968 Stratocaster* Hendrix played his version of "The Star-Spangled Banner" at Woodstock in 1969 on this guitar. From his death in 1970 until 1990 it was in the charge of Mitch Mitchell, drummer with The Jimi Hendrix Experience. In 1990, it was shown at the Fender Artist Center still with Jimi Hendrix's reverse stringing and burns from his cigarettes on the headstock. That year, it sold at Sotheby's for $198,000. However, Microsoft's Bill Gates' right-hand man Paul Allen is thought to have paid $2 million dollars for it in 1998.

3. $1.2–2 million (estimated value) *Bob Marley's custom-made Washburn 22 series Hawk* Considered a national asset by the Jamaican government, the guitar was one of only seven guitars in the reggae star's life. On November 21, 1971, Marley gave it to a guitar technician Gary Carlsen, saying: "Take it, you will understand later." Carlsen took this to mean that he should use the gift to make the world better in some way. He founded the charity "Different Journeys, One Destination" and offered the guitar as a prize in a fund-raising lottery.

Continued on p.40

PEAVEY EVH WOLFGANG

1996

The Wolfgang is a guitar that owes its existence to Eddie Van Halen; it is named after his son, who was, himself, named after Wolfgang Amadeus Mozart. When Van Halen fell out with Music Man guitars, it was natural that he should turn to Peavey, who already made his signature amplifier. The Wolfgang guitar that arose from this collaboration had an arched top, unlike the Music Man's flat top, and incorporated Van Halen's patented D-Tuna device, which allows the guitar's low E string to drop a tone to a D, despite the Floyd Rose locking vibrato. Later models reverted to the flat top. The Peavey EVH Wolfgang was discontinued in 2004.

Wolfgang
Amadeus
Mozart

1996 Peavey EVH
Wolfgang

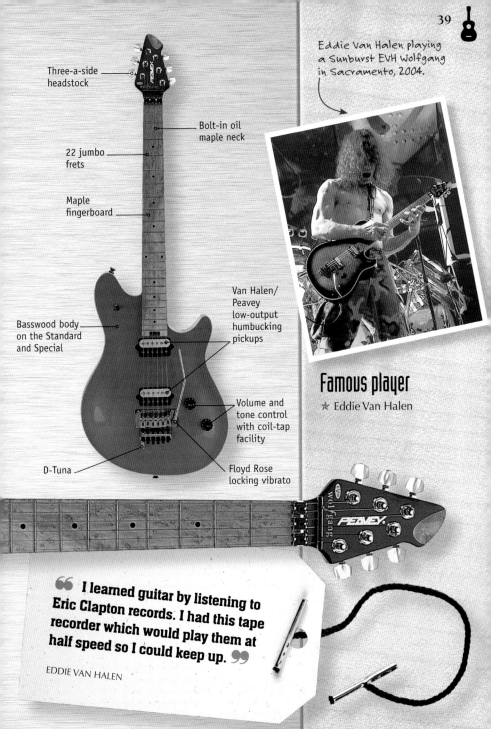

Three-a-side headstock

Bolt-in oil maple neck

22 jumbo frets

Maple fingerboard

Basswood body on the Standard and Special

Van Halen/ Peavey low-output humbucking pickups

Volume and tone control with coil-tap facility

D-Tuna

Floyd Rose locking vibrato

Eddie Van Halen playing a Sunburst EVH Wolfgang in Sacramento, 2004.

Famous player
★ Eddie Van Halen

> 66 I learned guitar by listening to Eric Clapton records. I had this tape recorder which would play them at half speed so I could keep up. 99

EDDIE VAN HALEN

The World's Ten Most Expensive Guitars, continued from p.37

4. $959,500 *Eric Clapton's Stratocaster hybrid "Blackie"*
Following the success of Jimi Hendrix, Eric Clapton decided to switch from a Gibson to a Stratocaster in 1970. He bought six vintage Strats from a guitar shop in Texas for $100 each. He gave one each to George Harrison, Pete Townshend, and Steve Winwood. Then he put together the best parts of the other three, naming the resulting guitar "Blackie" for its dark finish. Clapton played "Blackie" for the first time in January 1973, but had to retire it in 1985 due to problems with the neck. Nevertheless "Blackie" sold at auction for $959,000 in 2004.

5. $847,500 *Eric Clapton's 1964 Gibson ES0335 TDC*
Eric Clapton used this guitar while playing with The Yardbirds in 1964, but only rarely after that. When it was auctioned, it fetched the highest price ever paid for a Gibson.

6. $791,500 *Eric Clapton's C.F. Martin & Co., c. 1939*
Sold to raise money for the Crossroads Rehabilitation Center, which he founded on the Caribbean island of Antigua to help those addicted to drugs or alcohol.

FLAMENCO
Thanks to the Flamenco music of Andalucia, Spain became the center for guitar making—and playing—throughout the 19th century.

LUTHIERS
A guitar maker is sometimes known as a luthier, a term derived from the French for lute, from which the earliest guitars evolved.

Continued on p.41

THE ELECTRIC SITAR

After The Beatles made everything Indian fashionable in the late 1960s, Danelectro jumped on the bandwagon and produced the electric sitar. In fact, this was nothing more than a straightforward six-string electric guitar with extra sympathetic or drone strings added. A special "buzz bridge," developed by session musician Vincent Bell, gave it its distinctive sitar-like sound.

Hits that featured the electric sitar:

✪ "Monterey" (Eric Burdon and The Animals)

✪ "Signed, Sealed, Delivered" and "I Was Made to Love Her" (Stevie Wonder)

✪ "Hooked on a Feeling" (B.J. Thomas)

✪ "It's A Shame" (The Spinners)

✪ "Cry Like A Baby" (The Box Tops)

Artists that used the electric sitar:

✪ The Clash

✪ The Delphonics

✪ Genesis

✪ Guns N' Roses

✪ Lenny Kravitz

✪ Metallica

✪ Oasis

✪ Pearl Jam

✪ Santana

✪ REM

✪ The Stylistics

✪ Steely Dan

✪ Van Halen

✪ Yes

Continued from p.40

7. $623,500 *Stevie Ray Vaughan's 1965 Fender Composite Stratocaster "Lenny"*
In 1980, blues guitarist, Stevie Ray Vaughan, was given this Strat as a 26th birthday present by his wife, Lenny—and he named it after her. It was one of his favorite guitars and he used it extensively until his death in 1990. It has gold stickers on the body spelling out his initials SRV. In 2004 it was the first and only guitar ever released for sale by his estate, raising $623,500 at auction for the Crossroads Rehabilitation Center (see 6, p.40).

8. $570,000 *George Harrison and John Lennon's 1964 Gibson SG*
This guitar was used by The Beatles between 1966 and 1969. George Harrison used it when recording and touring with the album *Revolver*, while John Lennon used it during sessions for *The White Album*. It then came into the possession of George Peter Ham from the rock band Badfinger. After his death, it sold in 2004 at auction to an anonymous bidder, fetching $570,000.

A 1967 Coral electric sitar

Continued on p.42

The World's Ten Most Expensive Guitars, continued from p.41

9. $455,550 *Eric Clapton's Gold Leaf Stratocaster*
To celebrate Fender's 50th anniversary, Eric Clapton ordered a Custom Fender Strat plated in 23-carat gold, ostensibly as an art piece. It sold at Christie's for $455,000 in 1997.

10. $375,000 *1949 Fender Broadcaster prototype*
Leo Fender's prototype was the template for one of the most popular guitars ever made—the Fender Telecaster. It was sold for $375,000 in 1994, at that time, the highest price ever paid for a guitar.

The devil of a story

The story is that the blues guitarist Robert Johnson (1911–38) was taught to play the guitar by the devil one night at midnight at a crossroads near Dockery Plantation, once home to Charlie Patton "the father of the Delta Blues."

A Dyer Symphony harp-guitar

Steely sounds

Swedish immigrants Carl and August Larson were the first to design and build acoustic flat-top guitars especially for steel strings; they successfully applied for a patent in 1904. Their instruments were sold under numerous other people's brand names— Champion, Dyer, Euphonon, Maurer, Prairie State, Stahl, and Stetson. Their Dyer Symphony harp-guitars, based on a design by Chris Knutsen and made in the 1910s and 1920s, are among their finest achievements. Their company ceased to operate after the brothers died in the 1940s.

THE FIRST GUITAR HERO

One of the first guitarists to achieve fame internationally was the Italian Francesco Corbetta (1615–81). He was guitar teacher to Louis XIV of France and he dedicated his first book of music "La Guitare Royale" in 1674 to his patron, neglecting to mention that he had already dedicated the book to Charles II of England, another enthusiastic guitarist. It was full of tunes that even monarchs could master while managing the affairs of state. Corbetta is also thought to have written "Easie Lessons On The Guitar For Young Practitioners," which appeared in 1677, for a more general audience.

Francesco Corbetta

THE WOODLESS GUITAR

Some guitar makers in the Baroque period (c.1600–1750) dispensed with wood and made their guitars from tortoiseshell and ivory.

> 66 I'm no hell of a guitar player. But the one thing I've tried to do is to make the guitar sound like my voice. 99
>
> MUDDY WATERS

I'm off! You won't turn me into a guitar hero.

FENDER TELECASTER

1950

While Merle Travis, Paul Bigsby, Les Paul, and others had been experimenting with solid body designs for years, it was Leo Fender who came up with the first production guitar made from a solid plank. It had a detachable neck for ease of manufacture, a simple adjustable bridge, and twin pickups that gave the modern, twangy sound that found a role in country, jazz, blues, and heavy rock. It was less than two inches (50 cm) thick, a mere sliver compared to the guitars that had come before, and cutaway to make the last of its 21 frets easily accessible. It has been in continuous production since the day it was launched but reached its rock zenith with "Whole Lotta Love" by Led Zeppelin.

The pickup is set at an angle to improve volume across all the strings.

Maple neck with rosewood or integral maple fretboard

Solid ash or alder (other timbers have been used)

Simple three-saddle bridge (six-way bridges are available on some modern versions)

Two single-coil pickups (other versions have two Seth Lover-designed humbucker or one humbucker and one single-coil)

Three-way selector switch

Tone control

Volume control

1989 40th Anniversary Fender Telecaster

Famous players

* Muddy Waters
* Keith Richards
* Albert Lee
* Roy Buchanan
* Jimmy Bryant
* James Burton
* Danny Gatton
* Jimmy Page
* Albert Collins
* Brad Paisley
* Jonny Greenwood of Radiohead
* Graham Coxon of Blur
* Mike Stern

> 66 *I didn't think much of the Fender Telecaster when it came out. Anyone with a bandsaw could have put it together.* 99

TED McCARTY, GIBSON GENERAL MANAGER

RECORD BREAKER

The great jazz guitarist Lonnie Johnson (1889–1970) won a blues talent competition in St. Louis that ran for 18 weeks in 1925. He was awarded a recording contract with Okeh Records and recorded an incredible 130 records. B.B. King said that he was a greater influence than Robert Johnson.

A Rickenbacker Vibrola pickup

BEHIND YOU!

T-Bone Walker favored the Rickenbacker Vibrola pickup, even though he had at first found it hard to get used to. "It had an echo sound," he said. "I would hit a string and hear the note behind me."

Hey! Don't knock my bell!

66 ...since the invention of the guitar there are very few who study the vihuela. This is a great loss because... the guitar is nothing but a cow-bell, so easy to play, especially when strummed, that there is not a stable-boy who is not a musician of the guitar. 99

SEBASTIAN OROSCO (c.1600)

The Stradivarius from the National Music Museum

THE STRADIVARIUS GUITAR

The famous Italian violin maker Antonio Stradivari also made guitars. Four are known to have survived. They can be found at:

✪ The Rawlins Gallery of the National Music Museum, University of South Dakota, Vermillion, South Dakota.

✪ Ashmolean Museum, Oxford, England.

✪ The Musée de la Musique, Paris, France.

✪ A fourth is in a private Italian collection.

The Rawlins guitar has five double strings, typical of guitars of the 17th century, rather than the six single strings found on modern guitars. It is also smaller than today's instruments.

Air Guitar World Championships

Although air guitar competitions were originally a Swedish idea, the Air Guitar World Championships began in Oulu, Finland, in 1996 as a bit of a joke. Now more than 20 nations have joined in. They include: the United States, the United Kingdom, Canada, Australia, New Zealand, France, Germany, the Netherlands, Greece, Belgium, Norway, Switzerland, Japan, Thailand, Russia, Romania, and Brazil. And there are rules:

Each participant has to play air guitar on stage in two one-minute rounds:

Round 1: The air guitarist plays along to a track or medley of their own choosing.

Round 2: The air guitarist then plays along to a track picked by an organizer or competitor, which is usually kept secret until the round begins.

Other rules include:

Each participant plays alone—backing bands with real or air instruments are not allowed; roadies and groupies are allowed, but must leave the stage before the performance.

Participants have to play air guitar; other instruments are not allowed. Acoustic air guitars are permitted. Some events allow the use of a real guitar pick.

The jury use the same scoring system as in figure skating with each judge giving the contestant a score from 4.0 to 6.0 for:

Technical merit—how much the performance looks like the real playing, including accurate representation of fretwork, chords, picking, strumming, and other technical moves.

Stage presence—showmanship, charisma, and the ability to rock the audience.

Airness—a thoroughly subjective assessment of the performance in its own right.

SET-UPS OF THE STARS

Jimi Hendrix

Jimi Hendrix played his Stratocaster through Marshall, Sunn, and Fender amplifiers. For effects he used flanging, wah-wah, tape delay, Uni-Vibe Octavia, and Fuzz Face.

WHAT'S IN A NAME?

In the first few decades of the 20th century, American guitar makers often sold their guitars under other names:

- ✪ **Ditson of Chicago**: Bay State, Haynes Exelsior, Tilton
- ✪ **Lyon and Healy of Chicago**: Washburn, Boehm, Windsor
- ✪ **Larson of Chicago**: Maurer & Co, Stahl, Dyer, Stetson, Prairie State, Euphonon, Knutson
- ✪ **Martin of New York and Nazareth, Pennsylvania**: Martin & Schatz, Martin & Coupa, Martin & Bruno, H&J, Paramount, Ditson
- ✪ **Gibson of Kalamazoo**: Cromwell, Kel Kroyden, Recording King, Roy Smeck, Junior, Kalamazoo, Old Kraftsman
- ✪ **Kay of Chicago**: Kay Kraft, Mayflower, Orpheum, Recording King
- ✪ **Regal of Chicagos**: Regal, 20th Century, University, Bacon & Day
- ✪ **Weymann of Philadelphia**: Weymann, Keystone State, W&S, Varsity

Guitar Hero® includes bands such as Aerosmith®

In the comfort of your own home

In 2005 a music video game was released called *Guitar Hero®*. Players used a guitar-shaped controller to simulate playing lead, rhythm, and bass guitar along to rock tracks. Three years later, the would-be rock god could graduate to *Guitar Hero World Tour* where they joined a four-piece rock band. Adapted for various platforms, the game allows you to choose your genre. You can play along with bands such as Aerosmith, Metallica, Queen, Van Halen, and Foo Fighters. There are versions for the Nintendo DS and smartphones.

GUITAR HERO

AEROSMITH

GUILD STARFIRE

1960

In 1952, following a strike at Epiphone, former employee George Mann set up Guild Guitars with Alfred Dronge of the Sonola Accordion Company. More ex-Epiphone employees joined and they began making jazz guitars in their small New York factory. By 1960 they were ready to take on Gibson with the Starfire I with a single pickup, the Starfire II with twin pickups, and the Starfire III with twin pickups and a Bigsby vibrato. All three designs had a single cutaway. In 1963 they introduced the double cutaway with the IV, V, VI, and 12-stringed Starfire XII. Similar to the ES-175, they were hollow bodied with the ES-335 solid center block.

Guild Starfire III

Three-way toggle selector switch

Neck joins body at 16th fret on single-cutaway (18th fret on double-cutaway)

The Best of Lightnin' Hopkins

DeArmond pickups (Hagstrom humbuckers on later models)

Sapele mahogany or maple body

Bigsby vibrato

Two tone and two volume controls

Famous players

★ Buddy Guy

★ Lightnin' Hopkins

★ Alexis Korner

★ Jim Armstrong of Them

★ Dave Davies of The Kinks

BERT WEEDON WAS THE FIRST BRITISH GUITARIST IN THE U.K. SINGLES CHART, WITH "GUITAR BOOGIE SHUFFLE" IN 1959.

★ Bert Weedon

★ Robert Lockwood, Jr.

★ Tom Fogerty of Creedence Clearwater Revival

MAY THE FORCE...

Nylon strings exert a pull of 75 to 105 pounds (34–48 kg) on the guitar. Steel strings exert anything from 185 to 240 pounds (84–109 kg), depending on the gauge. The design of the guitar has to be strong enough to resist this force, but every time a structural bar is introduced, it risks interfering with a sounding bar. However, as steel strings produce a louder sound, volume is hardly a factor. This is why a steel-stringed model is easier to build than a classical guitar.

Unstrung

Early Baroque guitars had four or five courses for the strings. The six-string model was only developed around 1800.

A 1590 guitar with five courses

CHINESE PUZZLE

Antonio de Torres, the famous 19th-century Spanish guitar maker, made a guitar like a Chinese puzzle. It slotted together without glue. Disassembled, it would fit into a shoe box.

Wah-wah pedal

Fuzz box

Hendrix effects

To produce distortion, Jimi Hendrix used a Univibe adapted for him from an electric organ, a fuzz box, and a wah-wah pedal. This allowed him to stress a note within a run or give force and precision to a riff. He used a vibrola arm to alter the pitch and intensity of a note, control feedback and even imitate the whine of a bottleneck. He would get distortion on some strings, with others undistorted—leaving other musicians listening to his records to speculate on the identity of a second or third guitar player. His use and understanding of the equipment was second to none. His road manager Eric Barrett explained: "Jimi started out with 75 watts and ended up with six 4x12 Marshall cabinets, a 4x12 monitor, and four 100-watt Marshall tops, all souped-up and coupled-up through fuzz, wah-wah pedals, and a Univibe. He had a special box of gadgets and the fuzz and wah-wah pedals acted as preamps. If I tried to test his equipment, all I got was feedback, and I still don't understand to this day how he did it."

The Fifty Most Influential Guitar Albums

In 1994 *Guitarist* magazine came up with their "Top Fifty Most Influential Guitar Albums of All Time" (the main guitarist featured is named in brackets):

1 *Are You Experienced?*, The Jimi Hendrix Experience (Jimi Hendrix)

2 *Van Halen*, Van Halen (Eddie Van Halen)

3 *Led Zeppelin II*, Led Zeppelin (Jimmy Page)

4 *Disraeli Gears*, Cream (Eric Clapton)

5 Bluesbreakers, John Mayall's Bluesbreakers (Eric Clapton)

6 *Blow By Blow*, Jeff Beck

7 *Axis: Bold As Love*, The Jimi Hendrix Experience (Jimi Hendrix)

8 *In Rock*, Deep Purple (Ritchie Blackmore)

9 *The Shadows*, The Shadows (Hank Marvin)

10 *Appetite For Destruction*, Guns N' Roses (Slash)

11 *The Rolling Stones*, The Rolling Stones (Keith Richards)

12 *Surfing With the Alien*, Joe Satriani

13 *Dire Straits*, Dire Straits (Mark Knopfler)

14 *Nevermind*, Nirvana (Kurt Cobain)

15 *Volume 4*, Black Sabbath (Tony Iommi)

Continued on p.54

The Fifty Most Influential Guitar Albums, continued from p.53

Continued on p.55

SMASHING GUITARS

The Who were not just interested in distortion and feedback. Pete Townshend would take the guitar and rub it against the microphone stand, then smash it into the amplifier. He did this, not just for the sound it produced, but to make rock a performance art. "We smash our instruments, tear our clothes, and wreck everything," he said. "The expense doesn't worry us because that would get between us and our music." Touring they barely broke even. At one stage, Townshend was getting through 70 guitars a year and complained that he could not even put them down as a deductible expense as the tax man did not believe him. Despite having had six U.K. top five singles, by 1969 The Who were an estimated $2 million in debt. They were rescued by the album Tommy, which reached number one in the U.K. album charts and got to number four in the U.S.

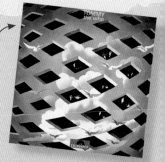

The album Tommy by The Who

> 66 When I'm on tour, I bring the Music Man. When something works you don't change it. I've been with her I think 11 years— we're a couple, her and me. 99

STEVE MORSE

Music Man

After Fender was bought by CBS in 1965, Leo Fender moved on to work with former employees Tom Walker and Forrest White at Music Man, where he designed the StingRay and Sabre guitars. Later they produced the Silhouette, favored by Keith Richards.

A 1976 Music Man StingRay

Continued from p.54

VOX PHANTOM XII STEREO

1963

The British company Vox originally made just organs and amps, but in 1961 they realized that there was a huge demand for guitars. Working with the Design Centre in London, they came up with the Phantom, with three single coils that looked like squared-off Strat pickups, a Bigsby-style vibrato, and a large scratchplate that virtually covered the five-sided body. The Mark VI had a teardrop-shaped body. Vox stopped making guitars in the 1970s, but the Phantom was reissued in the United States. Both the Phantom and the Teardrop are still manufactured by other makers. The Phantom can be seen on Joy Division's "Love Will Tear Us Apart" video.

Pickup detail

1964 Vox Phantom XII stereo

Spearhead headstock

Open-back tuners

Rosewood fingerboard (also available in ebony)

Bolt-on maple neck

Nickel-silver frets

Mahogany body (also available in maple and ash)

Three single-coil pickups

Five-way pickup selector

Effects buttons giving fuzz, tremolo, and repeat percussion

Mono/stereo switch

Volume and tone controls

·JOY DIVISION·
LOVE WILL TEAR US APART

Love Will Tear Us Apart by Joy Division

Famous players

★ Ian Curtis of Joy Division

★ Brian Jones

★ Tony Hicks of The Hollies

★ Chris Martin of Coldplay

★ Sterling Morrison of Velvet Underground

★ Lenny Davidson of The Dave Clark Five

VOX

Teardrop Mark VI (1965)

VOX

A classic sunburst-style Gibson Les Paul Junior

Junior guitars

Years before Fender came up with the idea of making versions of his guitars for younger players, Gibson had been making "junior" guitars for those just learning or younger artists who were short of cash. Even the Les Paul had its own student models. The Junior with one P-90 pickup came out in 1954; the Special with two in 1955. They did away with the expensive arched maple top and other frills, but they were made from quality materials and sounded good. Initially they had a single cutaway, but in 1958 changed to a double cutaway.

Whatever floats your boat

Musician Josh Pyke filmed the video for his song "Make You Happy" in a special boat created to the exact specifications of the Maton acoustic guitar that he performs with. The video was filmed at Rozelle Bay on October 9, 2008, in Sydney, Australia.

EARLIEST GUITARS

The first mention of anything remotely like a guitar appears in Italian and Spanish literature around 1300. There are references to the guitarra latina, guitarra moresca, and vihuela de mano. These instruments were a form of lute brought from North Africa to Spain by the Moors. The guitarra usually only had four strings and perhaps as few as five or six frets. It was primarily a plaything. It was the vihuela de mano with six or seven strings and ten or more frets that was the forerunner of the modern guitar.

A reproduction vihuela de mano made by the Spanish luthier Asier de Benito Guío

MAYBELLE'S METHOD

The Carter Family, America's leading country and western group from 1927 until the mid 1950s, blended their voices to the guitar, rather than the other way around. Maybelle Carter used a thumb-pick to create a melodic line on the bass string while producing the rhythm from chords play on the treble strings. She also used an up-down stroke, rather than the earlier down-brushing style.

The "father of country and western music" A. P. Carter sings with his wife Sara (on the autoharp) and her sister Maybelle (on guitar).

African mahogany, Indian rosewood, and Sitka spruce at the C.F. Martin saw mill in Pennsylvania.

TREAT IT WELL

Wood used for making guitars must be thoroughly seasoned so that the moisture from the living tree dries out. Air-drying is preferred to kiln-drying as it allows time for chemical changes to "cure" the wood. Guitar makers use wood seasoned for three to five years, though wood that has been seasoned for 20–30 years is preferred for top quality instruments. The wood must be cut as nearly as possible along the radius of the log. Otherwise it will twist and warp. It should be split rather than sawn.

> **" I took the guitar with me to the bathroom. Everywhere I went, I played it— because I loved it. "**
>
> CHET ATKINS

Orville Gibson

Working in his home workshop in Kalamazoo, Michigan, Orville Gibson (1856–1918) developed a new style of guitar with a top carved and arched like a violin. He patented his design. Soon his instruments were so popular that five Kalamazoo businessmen started the Gibson Mandolin-Guitar Manufacturing Company in 1902. Though a talented guitar maker, Gibson was not much of a businessman and seems to have worked only as a consultant to the company.

A GRETSCH STORY

In 1883 German immigrant Friedrich Gretsch (1855–95) opened a music shop in Brooklyn and made banjos, tambourines, and drums. When Friedrich died, his son Fred took over the company and moved into the Williamsburg district. By the 1930s the company was making lavish arch-top guitars to rival those of Gibson. Friedrich's grandson Fred Jr. took over in the 1950s, and Gretsch hollow-bodied electric guitars were given the endorsement of country star Chet Atkins. The Gretsch brand was also favored by Eddie Cochran, Roy Orbison, George Harrison, Pete Townshend, and Neil Young.

1957 Gretsch Country Gentleman

BIRTH OF THE BLUES

Southern-style guitar playing grew up alongside jazz in New Orleans at the beginning of the 20th century. According to one eyewitness: "Uptown in New Orleans they had a lot of country guitar players used to come to town and sit around and play. They hear bands play and they sit around in the barber shops and, if they catch the piece, they pick it out on the guitar."

MARTIN D-45

1933

In 1931 Martin launched a line of large acoustic guitars named after the huge British warship of World War I, the *Dreadnought*. They ran through the D-1, D-2, and D-18 until they figured they had perfected it with the D-28. Then along came the "Singing Cowboy" Gene Autry, who wanted a guitar like his hero Jimmie Rodgers' OOO-45, only in the larger Dreadnought style. Gene Autry's guitar had his name inlaid in pearl script in the fretboard. However, D-45s proved expensive to make and production was discontinued in 1941 when only 91 had been made. After World War II new versions came into production and they eventually sold over half-a-million guitars of this design.

1940 Martin D-45

Ebony
fretboard

Abalone pearl
inlays

Mahogany
neck

Rosewood body

Spruce
top

Gene Autry's playing was renowned throughout the world. Here he appears on a Guyanan stamp.

GUYANA $35

Gene Autry

Famous players

★ Gene Autry
★ Neil Young
★ Stephen Stills
★ Eric Clapton
★ Paul Simon
★ Marty Stuart
★ Joan Baez
★ Sting

DON'T FRET OVER THE PRICE

In 1994 Martin produced a facsimile of Gene Autry's 12-fret D-45, with a price tag of $23,000.

Blues techniques

Fingerpicking or Clawhammer: A pre-blues technique using the index finger, or the index and middle fingers to pick out the melody, while the thumb plays the bass string. White country players also adopted it, while Merle Travis and others used it as a basis for what became the Nashville sound.

The Hammer On: The string is plucked, then a finger-tip is brought down onto it behind a fret while it is ringing, producing a second, higher note. This technique, used by almost all American guitar players, both black and white, is thought to have been borrowed from the banjo.

The Pull Off: A stopped string is plucked, then the finger on the fret is moved to one side and raised, allowing the freed string to sound a second, lower note. It is the reverse of the Hammer On.

Whining, Bending, or Whamming: A stopped string is plucked, then pushed or pulled along the fret, causing the note to "whine" up in pitch. On modern guitars is it possible to "reverse whine" by straining the string before it is plucked, then relaxing it into its natural position. Rock guitarists have picked up on the whine to great effect and country players use it to mimic the sound of pedal steel guitars.

Choking or Damping: The edge of the palm is brought down on the bridge saddle, stopping the strings from ringing. Sometimes only the bass strings will be choked to mimic a bass. Texas blues guitarists also choke the bass strings by resting the ball of the thumb on them.

Left-hand Damping: The left hand can also be used for damping in two ways: on a fretted string, the stopping finger is raised slightly so the string pulls away from the fret; on an open string, the fleshy pad of the finger is brought down on the string, muffling it.

Bottleneck, Slide, Razor, or Knife Playing: In an attempt to imitate the Hawaiian guitar, African-American street musicians laid the guitar across their knees and stopped the strings with a bottle or a beer glass. Then only the bottleneck was used, slipped over the third or fourth finger, with the guitar being held upright, Spanish style. A razor, knife, or cigar tube is sometimes used. Later players used a lighter slide made from a polished metal tube.

Guitar player with a modern slide

FENDER PRECISION

The Audiovox electric bass made little impact outside the Pacific Northwest. It was only when Leo Fender came up with the Fender Precision Bass (P-Bass) in 1951 that the solid-bodied bass that could be played like a guitar really took off.

Fender Precision Bass

Eric Clapton

Clapton has played a Les Paul through a Marshall 12x12 combo, a Fender Champ named "Layla," and a Stratocaster through a Pignose portable amplifier and, more recently, a Stratocaster through Soldano and Fender-style amplifiers.

> " It's kinda funny. You just set out to play the electric guitar, and people think you want to change the world. "
>
> KEITH RICHARDS

PLUCKING METHODS

Early guitars were played with the little finger of the right hand resting on the bridge or soundboard while the strings were plucked in a pinching motion using the thumb and first two fingers. As the guitar grew larger, the arm rested on the top of the guitar's body leaving the hand free to float over the strings. A warm sound could be produced by plucking the strings over the sound hole; a brighter, metallic sound could be made if they were plucked near the bridge.

By the 16th century two distinct styles of playing the guitar had evolved, which persist to this day: Rasgueado—chordal strumming favored by players of the five-string guitar, and Punteado—finger-picking individual notes, favored by players of the four-string guitar.

It was only in the 19th century that the other fingers came into play, and controversy raged about whether the strings should be plucked with the nails or the tips of the fingers. Then two other techniques evolved: Tirando—where the fingers of the right hand return to the raised position after the string has been plucked, and Apoyando—where the fingers come to rest on the next string.

The price of solidity

The Singerland Model 401 is generally regarded as the first solid-body guitar. It went on sale in 1936 for $135.

> 66 **Leo's beliefs and my beliefs were terribly similar. We just had different ideas about the sounds we wanted to create.** 99

LES PAUL ON LEO FENDER

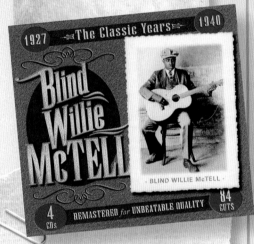

Blind Willie McTell

Born in Thompson, Georgia, around 1900, Blind Willie McTell escaped poverty by his ability on the 12-string guitar. However, in the 1920s he quit music to go to school. But he soon found that his callused fingers prevented him from learning Braille and he returned to music and a recording career that continued until 1956.

Top 100 Guitar Players of All Genres

In a list compiled by the website digitaldreamdoor.com, guitarists were picked for their innovation, respect from other guitarists, influence on other players, and overall impact on the guitar world.

1 Andrès Segovia (classical)
2 Django Reinhardt (jazz)
3 Chet Atkins (country)
4 Jimi Hendrix (rock)
5 Paco de Lucia (flamenco)
6 Agustin Barrios Mangore (classical)
7 Ramon Montoya (flamenco)
8 Julian Bream (classical)
9 Charlie Christian (jazz)
10 B.B. King (blues)
11 T-Bone Walker (blues)
12 Merle Travis (country)
13 Wes Montgomery (jazz)
14 John Williams (classical)
15 Michael Hedges (contemporary fingerstyle)
16 Lonnie Johnson (blues)
17 Eddie Lang (jazz)
18 Lenny Breau (jazz)
19 John McLaughlin (fusion)
20 Joe Pass (jazz)
21 Sabicas (flamenco)
22 Blind Blake (ragtime, blues)
23 Robert Johnson (blues)
24 John Fahey (contemporary fingerstyle, folk, etc)
25 Davey Graham (British folk, contemporary fingerstyle)
26 Doc Watson (folk)
27 Danny Gatton (rockabilly, etc)

Continued on p.70

IBANEZ JEM

1987

The Japanese guitar makers Ibanez had been copying European and American designs until, in 1977, Gibson's owners Norlin Music successfully sued Ibanez's parent company Hoshino over the headstock design of one of their models. Consequently, Ibanez began looking for original designs of its own. First it produced the Iceman, which found favor with Kiss front man Paul Stanley. By the mid 1980s, it had secured the endorsement of Frank Zappa and David Lee Roth.

Ibanez then approached Steve Vai (Zappa's former guitarist), who simply gave them his main instrument, put together by Joe Despagni of JEM Guitars, and told them to make one like it. When they delivered the prototype, he made some changes—a lighter basswood body, instead of heavier maple, and rosewood, instead of maple on the fingerboard, DiMarzio pickups, and a scalloped fingerboard from the 21st fret upward. The guitar that emerged was the Ibanez JEM 777.

1997 90th Anniversary Ibanez JEM

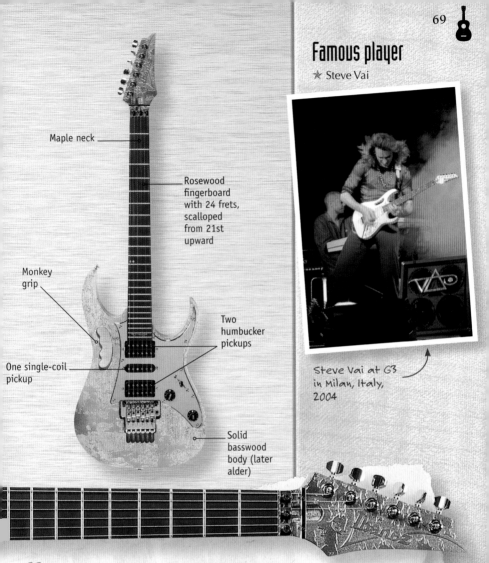

Famous player

★ Steve Vai

Maple neck

Rosewood fingerboard with 24 frets, scalloped from 21st upward

Monkey grip

Two humbucker pickups

One single-coil pickup

Solid basswood body (later alder)

Steve Vai at G3 in Milan, Italy, 2004

66 **I handed them my prototype and said: 'Here's the guitar I want—make me one exactly like it.' And I got a guitar back in three weeks that was just great… duplicating the one guitar I really like.** 99

STEVE VAI ON THE IBANEZ JEM

Top 100 Guitar Players
of All Genres, continued from p.67

28 Adrian Legg (contemporary fingerstyle)
29 Narciso Yepes (classical)
30 Laurindo Almeida (Brazilian)
31 Les Paul (jazz)
32 Christopher Parkening (classical)
33 Pat Metheny (fusion, jazz)
34 Sol Ho'opi'i (Hawaiian)
35 Jeff Beck (rock)
36 Eddie Van Halen (rock)
37 Ritchie Blackmore (rock)
38 Alexandre Lagoya and Ida Presti (classical)
39 Phil Keaggy (rock, contemporary fingerstyle)
40 Allan Holdsworth (fusion)
41 Baden Powell (Brazilian)
42 Nino Ricardo (flamenco)
43 George Van Eps (jazz)
44 Jim Hall (jazz)
45 Ed Bickert (jazz)
46 Kenny Burrell (jazz)
47 Franco (soukous, rumba)
48 Carlos Paredes (fado)
49 Freddie Green (jazz)
50 Eric Clapton (rock, blues)
51 Jimmy Page (rock)
52 Albert King (blues)
53 Hank Garland (country, jazz)
54 Chuck Berry (rock)
55 Tommy Emmanuel (contemporary fingerstyle)
56 Leo Kottke (contemporary fingerstyle)
57 Tony Iommi (rock)
58 King Bennie Nawahi (Hawaiian)
59 Enver Izmailov (fusion)
60 Stanley Jordan (jazz, fusion)
61 Robert Fripp (avant-garde, rock)

Continued on p.71

> ❝ *It's very simply the best guitar you can buy today.* ❞
>
> EDDIE VAN HALEN ON A KRAMER PROMO IN THE MID-1980S

"Little Almond"

The mandolin is a close relative of the guitar and plays alongside it in country and bluegrass bands. The name comes from the Italian for "little almond." It is found in various forms around the world, particularly in South America, where a variant known as the bandolim has five pairs of strings instead of the mandolin's four.

Silent guitar

The silent guitar is designed to make no noise—up to a point. The body is made so that it does not amplify the vibration of the strings, leaving them, effectively, silent. However, the vibrations are picked up by a piezoelectric pickup. Three types of silent guitar have been produced:

○ **Full-sized**: The first full-sized silent guitar was the Gibson Chet Atkins SST. It has been played by Dave Matthews, among others.

○ **Small-bodied**: As the size of the body makes no difference to the sound, small-bodied versions were made. As they could be played through headphones without disturbing other people, they were a great boon to travelers.

○ **Skeleton guitar**: In this instrument, what remained of the guitar body was reduced to a frame that could rest on the knee. This could even be detached, making it the ultimate portable guitar.

An Epiphone SST, the modern successor to the Gibson Chet Atkins SST

Continued from p.70

62 Oscar Moore (jazz)
63 Ernest Ranglin (ska, jazz)
64 Gabby Pahinui (Hawaiian slack key)
65 Vishwa Mohan Bhatt (Indian)
66 Johnny Smith (jazz)
67 Roy Buchanan (rock)
68 Bill Frisell (fusion, jazz)
69 Manuel Barrueco (classical)
70 Kazuhito Yamashita (classical)
71 Jimmy Bryant (country, jazz)
72 Duane Allman (rock, blues)
73 James Burton (rockabilly)
74 Freddie King (blues)
75 Elmore James (blues)
76 Earl Hooker (blues)
77 Juanjo Dominguez (tango, etc)
78 Roberto Grela (tango)
79 Mother Maybelle Carter (country)
80 Stevie Ray Vaughan (blues)
81 Steve Vai (rock)
82 Yngwie Malmsteen (rock)
83 Steve Morse (rock)
84 Eric Johnson (rock)
85 Tony Rice (bluegrass)
86 Bola Sete (Brazilian, folk fusion)
87 Richard Thompson (British folk)
88 John Renbourn (British folk)
89 Bert Jansch (British folk)
90 Buddy Guy (blues)
91 Steve Cropper (r&b, blues)
92 Robert White/Joe Messina/Eddie Willis (r&b)
93 Scotty Moore (rockabilly)
94 Barney Kessel (jazz)
95 Tal Farlow (jazz)
96 Jimmy Raney (jazz)
97 Howard Roberts (jazz)
98 George Benson (jazz, r&b)
99 Debashish Bhattacharya (Indian)
100 Ry Cooder (blues, etc)

Amplifier advances

Amplifiers of the 1930s had small speakers with an output that rarely exceeded 10 or 15 watts, but by the 1940s musicians could buy huge bandstand set-ups such as the Epiphone Electar Zephyr.

The Epiphone Electar Zephyr valve amp, 1946

Leather guitar

Gary Kramer has made a "leather guitar." The guitar body is wrapped in leather like the steering wheel of an expensive car.

THE DREADNOUGHT

In 1916 Frank Henry Martin (1865–1948), the grandson of C.F. Martin (1796–1873), the company's founder, developed the large-bodied Dreadnought, named after the British World War I battleship. Originally they were made exclusively for the Ditson store. But when Ditson went out of business, Martin produced a range for more general sale. The legendary D-45 Dreadnought was originally made for the "Singing Cowboy" film-star Gene Autry, who played a major role in popularizing the acoustic guitar in the 1930s. Its production was discontinued in 1942, but was resumed in 1968 when it became popular with folk and country artists.

1933 Martin D-45

THE SUPERSTRAT

In 1977 Grover Jackson was employed in Wayne Charvel's guitar repair shop in Azusa, California, fixing replacement necks and bodies. Two years later Jackson bought the business and moved to San Dimas, California, where he designed and built the "superstrat." It had a Stratocaster-shaped body, a sleek bolt-on neck, and a Fender-style headstock. What made it "super" was the flashy paint job, which became a specialty of the company.

Banjo strings

Chuck Berry borrowed a trick from older bluesmen, who had abandoned the sixth string, moved the remaining strings down one, and then substituted a banjo string for the top E. With three unwound strings and all the strings of a lighter gauge, it was easier to bend the strings. The set-up did not become commercially available until the Fender Rock 'n' Roll set in the early 1960s.

MUSIC MAN SILHOUETTE

1986

In 1984 string manufacturers Ernie and Sterling Ball bought the guitar designs of Music Man, a company founded in the 1970s by Leo Fender and Tom Walker. They came up with a light guitar with a vibrant tone. It had a slim neck, finished in gunstock oil to make it easy to play. It was relatively rigid, had a long heel, and five bolts holding the neck in place. And it has a truss rod that could be adjusted without removing the neck or strings. Among guitarists, the Silhouette was an instant hit, with signature models being produced for Albert Lee and Eddie Van Halen among others.

Pickup detail

1988 Music Man Silhouette

Fender "four and two" tuner layout

Bolt-on maple neck

Double cutaway

Deep-set heel with five bolts

Solid ash body

Three single-coil pickups on early models

Volume and tone controls

Steve Morse at the Roxy Theater, Hollywood, California, 1999

Famous players

- ⭐ Keith Richards
- ⭐ Ronnie Wood
- ⭐ Steve Morse
- ⭐ Albert Lee
- ⭐ Eddie Van Halen

MUSIC MAN

Silhouette

To me, the Music Man guitar is the best new design of the last 20 years. It's the only modern classic.

KEITH RICHARDS

GREATEST METAL GUITARISTS

The following list of the top guitarists playing in the heavy metal genre is based on the ranking compiled by the website digitaldreamdoor.com:

1 Tony Iommi (Black Sabbath)
2 Yngwie Malmsteen (Solo)
3 Randy Rhoads (Ozzy, Quiet Riot)
4 Ritchie Blackmore (Deep Purple, Rainbow)
5 Steve Vai (Dave Lee Roth, Solo, Whitesnake)
6 Michael Schenker (MSG, UFO, Scorpions)
7 Marty Friedman (Megadeth, Cacophony, Solo)
8 Uli John Roth (Scorpions, Solo)
9 Adrian Smith (Iron Maiden, Dickinson, Psycho Motel, ASAP, Urchin)
10 Glenn Tipton (Judas Priest, Solo)
11 Dave Murray (Iron Maiden)
12 Dimebag Darrell (Pantera, Damageplan)
13 Chuck Schuldiner (Death, Control Denied)
14 Dave Mustaine (Megadeth)
15 Kirk Hammett (Metallica)
16 Paul Gilbert (Mr Big, Racer X)
17 George Lynch (Dokken, Lynch Mob, Solo)
18 Alex Skolnick (Testament, Trans Siberian Orchestra, Savatage)
19 Jason Becker (Dave Lee Roth, Cacophony)
20 John Petrucci (Dream Theater, Liquid Tension Exp)

Music soothes the savage breast

As a youth the Brazilian composer Heitor Villa-Lobos (1887–1959) went on the road with his guitar to learn the folk music of his native country. He later told the fanciful story that he was captured by cannibals in the Amazon rainforests, but avoided being eaten by enchanting the would-be diners with the quality of his playing.

66 ...the guitar is an immensely beautiful and valuable instrument in our musical heritage in its sounds and its ability to evoke atmosphere... The guitar has a uniquely evocative character in its ability to cast a spell. 99

JULIAN BREAM

Julian Bream, January 1970

THREAT OF EXPULSION

In the late 1940s the eminent British classical guitarist Julian Bream was threatened with expulsion from London's Royal College of Music for practicing his guitar on the premises. In England at that time, the guitar was associated with skiffle groups—not the sort of instrument a gentleman studying "serious music" should be playing at all.

GOOD VIBRATIONS

Steel strings are more efficient vibrators than those made from nylon. While a plucked nylon string will produce a note with six to ten overtones, a steel string will produce 40 to 50, perhaps even more. As the air that carries the sound to our ears damps the overtones at a different rate, they become out of tune with each other, giving the steel strings a twanging, jangly sound.

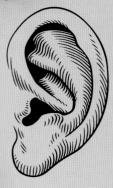

V-head

Dean Zelinsky founded Dean Guitars in Evanston, Illinois, in 1977. His early designs were much like Gibsons. To make them distinctive, he added a unique V-shaped headstock, which carried his famous winged logo.

CANALEJAS DE PUERTO REAL

GRABACIONES
❀ DISCOS ❀
PIZARRA

AÑO 1930

The day the music died

The legendary flamenco guitarist Manolo de Huelva (c.1892–1968) grew secretive as he grew older. He would play only at private functions, recorded little, and refused to perform his best material if other guitarists were present. As a consequence, his music died with him.

> 66 *Les Paul is the one really. We wouldn't be anywhere if he hadn't invented the electric guitar.* 99
>
> JIMMY PAGE

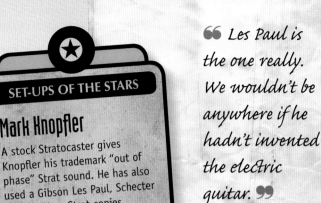

The first electric lap steel guitar, the "Frying Pan," created in 1931 by George Beauchamp

PUMP UP THE VOLUME

The problem with the acoustic guitar was that, in a noisy club or playing in a jazz band, it was simply not loud enough. However, following the invention of the telephone, the phonograph, the radio, and the amplifier, it was natural that electricity should be applied to the problem. In the late 1920s, Lloyd Loar of the Gibson company experimented with electric pickups, while the Dobro guitar company were also early pioneers. Then George Beauchamp of the National String Instrument Company linked a single-string test guitar with the pickup from a Brunswick electric phonograph. He then quit National and went into business with his friend Adolph Rickenbacker. In 1936, Gibson introduced their first electric Hawaiian and Spanish guitars. These were loud enough to hold their own against a trumpet or a saxophone and were taken up by Charlie Christian, T-Bone Walker, and Les Paul.

PARKER FLY

1992

Luther Ken Parker believed that traditional guitar construction inhibited the vibration of the strings and dulled the transference of the tone to the pickups. So he threw the rule book away. He slimmed down the solid body to ½ inch (13 mm) at its thinnest, 1½ inches (38 mm) at its thickest. In comparison, the Telecaster is nearly 2 inches (50 mm) thick all over. The basswood neck and back of Parker's design are reinforced with a skin of glass and carbon fiber. Acoustic pickup guru Larry Fisherman used twin humbuckers to produce both acoustic and electric tone—and a mixture of the two. Since its launch, the company have introduced many variants: the nylon-stringed Spanish Fly, the mahogany-bodied Classic, the 22-fret NiteFly, the all-mahogany Fly Mojo, the Mojo Singlecut with Seymour Duncan pickups and an optional flamed maple top, and the Mojo Snakeskin with genuine snakeskin bonded to the front.

Parker Fly Deluxe in ice blue burst

Sperzl locking tuners

24 stainless steel frets (22 on NiteFly)

Basswood or mahogany neck

Glass and carbon fiber fingerboard

Multifinger heelless neck joint

Thin glass and carbon fiber skin on back and neck

Carved poplar body

Aluminum vibrato bridge with stainless steel piezo-loaded saddles

Twin Di Marzio custom-wound pickups

3-way mag pickup selection with push-pull coil tap

Famous players

★ The Edge

★ Eddie Van Halen

★ Keith Richards

★ Joni Mitchell

★ Merle Haggard

★ Adrian Belew

★ Joe Walsh of The Eagles

★ Phil Campbell of Motorhead

★ Reeves Gabrels of Tin Machine

Joni Mitchell's album Both Sides Now

❝ *My Parker has taken a hell of a beating and is still going strong.* ❞

REEVES GABRELS ON THE PARKER FLY

AN INSTRUMENT OF EQUALITY

The guitarra was played as much by women as by men. In Spain strolling players would set up in the courtyards of large houses, where they were sure to get a big audience, who were often vociferous and rowdy. Meanwhile the courtly vihuela de mano was played both by aristocrats and the professional musicians they employed.

The Log

Sideman with Bing Crosby and Nat King Cole, Les Paul (1915–2009) began experimenting with designs for an electric guitar in 1928. He grew dissatisfied with the sound of the acoustic guitar with an electric pickup bolted on. Working in his own apartment in Queens, New York, he attached the neck, bridge, and pickup of a guitar to a solid piece of four-by-four maple to create "The Log." In a production version in 1940, he stuck the log between two halves of the body of an Epiphone hollow-body guitar he had sawn down the middle.

MARSHALLED SOUNDS

In 1960 Jim Marshall (1923–), who ran
a music store in London, began producing
amplifiers to compete with the more expensive
imported Fenders. The resulting Marshall
amplifiers changed the sound of the guitar.
In 1965 Eric Clapton plugged his Les Paul into
a Marshall 45-watt amplifier. The following
year, Jimi Hendrix played his Stratocaster
through a Marshall stack. The Marshall
amplifier even persuaded classical guitarist
Andrès Segovia to try the electric guitar.

ROYAL SERENADE

Henri II of France (1519–59) set
a new fashion by serenading his
beautiful mistress Diane de
Poitiers with music played on the
guitar. It seems that Henry VIII of
England (1491–1547) also took
to the instrument. Among his
collection of musical instruments,
there were four "guitterons with
four cases… they are called
Spanish Vialles." Charles II of
England (1630–85) was a guitar
fan, while two of the daughters
of Louis XIV (1638–1715) had
guitars made for them.

Marshall amplifiers

If I don't like the guitar, I can always have its head chopped off!

Henry VIII of England

MOVE ASIDE MANDOLINS

In its early years, the Gibson Mandolin-Guitar Manufacturing Company concentrated on making mandolins. However, in 1919, the year after Orville Gibson's death, the company took on Lloyd Loar (1886–1946). In 1923 he revolutionized the company's produce range with the L-5—the first arch-top guitar with violin-style "f-holes" and a raised pickguard. It was popular with dance bands. Around 1936, Gibson produced the ES 150 ("ES" stood for "Electric Spanish"). Thanks to Charlie Christian and T-Bone Walker, it became their most popular model.

Gibson ES 150

TOP 20

GREATEST R&B/SOUL GUITARISTS

The top twenty R&B/Soul guitarists listed here were selected by visitors to the website digitaldreamdoor.com:

1 Steve Cropper (60s sessions, Booker T & the MGs)
2 Bo Diddley
3 B.B. King
4 Ernie Isley (The Isley Brothers)
5 Chuck Berry
6 Jimmy Nolen (The JBs)
7 Albert King
8 Curtis Mayfield (The Impressions)
9 Robert Cray
10 Mickey "Guitar" Baker (50s session guitarist)
11 Eddie Hazel (Funkadelic)
12 Peter Tosh (The Wailers)
13 Joe Messina (The Funk Brothers, Motown sessions)
14 Nile Rodgers (Chic)
15 Leo Nocentelli (The Meters)
16 Robert White (The Funk Brothers, Motown sessions)
17 Marv Tarplin (The Miracles)
18 Sister Rosetta Tharpe
19 Lowman Pauling (The "5" Royales)
20 Snooks Eaglin

Get rid of that fretbuzz

Whether you are playing single notes or chords, the expert advice is to press down on the string as close to the fretwire as possible. This minimizes unpleasant "fretbuzz" sounds. Pressing against the edge of the fret also reduces the pressure required, allowing for a lighter touch and more fluent playing. And, unless you are playing more than one note, you should use the tip of the finger rather than the fleshy pad for a cleaner sound.

66 **The whole group [The Byrds] went to see A Hard Day's Night. George was playing a Rickenbacker 12-string so I went out and bought one.** 99

ROGER McGUINN

RICKENBACKER 360-12

1964

Rickenbacker guitars were overshadowed by Gibson and Fender in the early 1960s. But when The Beatles embarked on their first U.S. tour in 1964, the company seized its opportunity. Rickenbacker boss Francis C. Hall knew that John Lennon already played a Rickenbacker 325, while George Harrison had bought a solid-bodied 425 when he had visited his sister in Miami the previous year. Meeting with the group, Hall gave Lennon an updated 325, Paul McCartney a left-handed bass, and Harrison a 360-12—only the second ever built and the first with a new tuning system. This innovatory 12-string guitar retained a standard headstock with the second six tuners facing backwards, as on a classical guitar, and used the Spanish-style slotted design. The 360-12 would go on to define the future sound of The Beatles, The Byrds, and REM. It was heard on The Beatles' "A Hard Day's Night," The Byrd's "Mr. Tambourine Man," and REM's "Smiley Happy People."

A 1965-design Rickenbacker 360-12 made in 1993

Conventional headstock to preserve balance

Glued-in maple neck

Rosewood fingerboard with dot markers (earlier versions have shark-fin markers)

Maple semihollow body carved out from the rear with glued-on back

Twin high-output "toaster top" pickups

Two-tiered white pickguard

Two volume and two tone controls (plus a fifth "blend" knob added later)

Red Hot Chili Peppers' Californication

Famous players

★ George Harrison

★ Roger McGuinn

★ Brian Jones

★ Peter Buck

★ Tom Petty

★ Pete Townshend

★ The Edge

★ John Frusciante of the Red Hot Chili Peppers

★ Jeff Buckley

Rickenbacker

66 The delicate body shape, the lightness of the woodwork, the carefully constructed craftsman-like neck all contribute to a guitar that is utterly different in every way from all other makes. I often feel that Rickenbackers are like violins rather than guitars. 99

PETE TOWNSHEND

OUT OF THE FRYING PAN

The Rickenbacker "Frying Pan" was a lap guitar with the strings stopped by a metal bar or slider, Hawaiian-style. It was first produced in 1932. Two years later Rickenbacker produced two Spanish electric models—one hollow, the other solid-bodied. After 1953, when the company was bought up by Francis C. Hall, who had previously distributed Fender guitars in California, it came up with radical new designs with skinny necks and deep cutaways. In 1959 and 1960, Belgian jazzman Toots Thielemans played a Rickenbacker at a number of concerts in West Germany. A young guitarist named John Lennon sought out a thin hollow-bodied Model 325. Then George Harrison bought a Rickenbacker 425. Pete Townshend of The Who and Roger McGuinn of The Byrds also favored Rickenbackers.

Vietnam veterans

While the Vietnam War raged, Hang-Don guitars were being made in that battle-scarred country. The designs were loosely based on Fenders, but they are said to be unplayable due to their unsuitable microphone pickups.

Rickenbacker 425

SET-UPS OF THE STARS

Jeff Beck

Beck has played Telecasters, Stratocasters, and Les Pauls through Marshall or Fender amplifiers. Effects include wah-wah, delay, and ProCo Rat.

Davoli
Krundaal
Bikini

MOTORCYCLE PARTS

The most eccentric Italian guitar designs come from Antonio "Wandré" Pioli (1926–2004), a luthier, who was into motorbikes as well as guitars. Indeed, the hardware styling is based on motorcycle parts while the finishing comes from his artist's eye for color and texture. His 1962 model, the Bikini, has the profile of a bike, with the accompanying amplifier and speaker forming the "back wheel."

66 I've used my black 360 Rick on every record we've ever done. It's my main guitar. I bought it new, beat it up, splattered blood on it, and now it's my guitar. You play a guitar for ten years and it's almost a part of you. 99

PETER BUCK OF REM

Bargain electrics

The 1936 Gibson E-150, arguably the first commercially successful Spanish-style electric guitar, was designated the "150" because it cost $150, including an EH-150 amplifier and cable.

Gibson E-150

MR. GUITAR

"The Country Gentleman" Chet Atkins (1924–2001) was also known as "Mr. Guitar." Although he picked up nine Country Music Association Instrumentalist of the Year Awards—on top of his 15 Grammys, including "Lifetime Achievement,"—he was inducted into the Rock and Roll Hall of Fame only after his death, in 2002.

Chet Atkins

Play in a Day

In 1957 the British guitarist Bert Weedon published *Play in a Day*, which sold two million copies worldwide. Among those who have acknowledged that Weedon helped them learn to play the guitar are John Lennon, Paul McCartney, Eric Clapton, Mark Knopfler, Brian May, Pete Townshend, Sting, and Mike Oldfield.

PLAY IN A DAY

Bert Weedon's GUITAR GUIDE
TO MODERN GUITAR PLAYING

CHAPPELL & CO. LTD.

GREATEST ACOUSTIC GUITARISTS

The following list, from digitaldreamdoor.com, is of musicians whose main instrument has been or is now the acoustic guitar:

1 Michael Hedges
2 Leo Kottke
3 Chet Atkins
4 Phil Keaggy
5 John Fahey
6 Adrian Legg
7 Merle Travis
8 John Renbourn
9 Bert Jansch
10 Tommy Emmanuel
11 Norman Blake
12 Doc Watson
13 Preston Reed
14 Laurence Juber
15 Martin Simpson
16 Don Ross
17 Nick Webb
18 Pierre Bensusan
19 Jorma Kaukonen
20 Sandy Bull

BRITAIN GETS THE BLUES

In the 1960s British guitar bands began to re-export the American blues music that they had been listening to. Rolling Stones guitarist Keith Richards had taken an early interest in rock 'n' roll music "…then I started to get into where it was coming from. [Big Bill] Broonzy first. He and Josh White were considered to be the only living black bluesmen still playing. So let's get that together, I thought, that can't be right. Then I started to discover Robert Johnson and those cats… The other half of me was listening to all that rock and roll, Chuck Berry, and saying yeah, yeah."

A Gibson Flying V with a Bigsby vibrato tailpiece

The whammy bar

The tremolo arm is also known as the "whammy bar," after blues-rock guitarist Lonnie Mack's use of the Bigsby vibrato tailpiece on his Gibson Flying V on the Top 30 instrumental hit "Wham."

EPIPHONE CASINO

1958

When Gibson bought the Epiphone company in 1957, it designed the Casino and its sister guitar the Riviera to be built alongside its ES-335 and ES-330 models. In fact, the Casino's designation was ES-230. It was a hollow, slimline model with two f-holes. The body is made of laminates, steam-pressed to create its arched appearance. It carried two Gibson P-30 pickups. Although Epiphone were widely seen as the poor relation of Gibson,

The Beatles took to the Casino. Paul McCartney bought one in 1964. George Harrison got one the following year, and had the pickguard removed and a Bigsby vibrato added. John Lennon then followed suit, but had his stripped and lacquered. It can be heard on "Ticket to Ride" and "Another Girl" (*Help!*), "Drive My Car" (*Rubber Soul*), "Paperback Writer" and "Taxman" (*Revolver*), and "Good Morning" (*Sergeant Pepper*).

1995 Epiphone Casino

Headstock set at 17-degree (later versions 14-degree) angle

Rectangular position markers (the earliest models had pearloid dots)

Rosewood fingerboard

Glued-in mahogany neck

Slimline semi-acoustic body made from laminated maple (early models have a spruce top)

Neck joins body at 16th fret

Twin P-90 pickups (earliest models had a single P-90 mounted in the middle)

Tortoiseshell pickguard with "E" logo (later models had a white pickguard)

Three-way selector switch

Two volume and two tone controls

(What's the Story) Morning Glory? by Oasis

Famous players

* Paul McCartney
* George Harrison
* John Lennon
* Paul Weller
* Noel Gallagher of Oasis

> 66 *If I had to choose one electric guitar, it would be this.* 99

PAUL McCARTNEY ON THE EPIPHONE CASINO

THE GITTERN

An early relative of the guitar was the gittern. This instrument, popular from the 13th until the 16th centuries, had a fretted neck, gut strings, and a flat back, and parallel sides. The only surviving example was carved from a single piece of wood. The early gittern had two sound holes, like a violin, although later versions had a single hole decorated with an ornate carved rose. It is mentioned in "The Pardoner's Tale," one of Chaucer's *Canterbury Tales*, written in the late 14th century. It tells of a raucous bar-room gig:

In Flanders whilom was a compaignye
Of yonge folk that haunteden folye
As riot, hazard, stywes, and taverns
Wher as with harpes, lutes and gyternes
They daunce and pleyen at dees bothe day and nyght.

> " The guitar is a small orchestra. "
>
> ANDRÉS SEGOVIA

MUSTACHES

Some early guitars had "mustaches"—decorative fretwork curlicues on the soundboard at the end of the bridge.

David Crowder, a modern "keytarist"

HAMMERED GUITAR

In the 18th century, there was a brief fashion for guitars that had a small keyboard added to the lower end of the soundbox. This activated a series of small hammers that struck the string, producing the desired note. Modern "ketars" are based on synthesizer technology.

Frontpiece from Luis Milán's vihuela book, El Maestro

Early works

Luis Milán's *El Maestro*, published in 1535, was the first book about the vihuela de mano, an early guitar. An illustration in it shows an instrument shaped like a guitar with six courses of strings, tuned like a lute. Twenty years later *Declaraciónde Instrumentos Musicales* by Juan Bermudo (c.1510–c.1565) also shows a seven-string version, although only fragments of music for the seven-stringed instrument survive from that time.

Synthetic Segovia

During the 1940s the great classical guitarist Andrés Segovia was touring the United States when he mentioned the difficulty of getting gut strings in America to General Lindeman of the British Embassy. A month later Lindeman presented Segovia with some nylon strings that he had obtained from DuPont, but these produced a slightly metallic timbre, which he felt could be corrected. DuPont were unwilling to manufacture nylon guitar strings commercially, but agreed to provide the necessary plastic material to anyone who was undertaking the task.

Danish immigrant Albert Augustine, a guitar maker Segovia had met some time before, was persuaded to have a go. It took him three years. Having produced satisfactory treble strings, he sent them to Segovia, who was performing in Washington. As luck would have it, he broke one of his precious Pirastro gut strings, replaced it with one of Augustine's nylon ones, and was delighted with the result. Augustine then turned to bass strings and these also received Segovia's endorsement.

Paul Reed Smith said: 'Hey Carlos, I want to send you this guitar and if you don't like it, send it back. If you do like it, then call me.' And since I played that guitar, I can't go back to anything else.

CARLOS SANTANA

IN HIDING

When archivist John Lomax and his assistant first tried to record Muddy Waters in his early days in Mississippi, Waters hid, fearing they were policemen trying to arrest him for making illegal liquor.

Coke-bottle head

Early Danelectro guitars had a distinctive headstock that was shaped like a Coca-Cola bottle.

A 1956 Danelectro U2

TOP 100 GUITAR SOLOS

Guitar magazine's readers' poll of the "Top 100 Guitar Solos of All Time" resulted in the following published rankings:

1 "Hotel California," The Eagles (Joe Walsh And Don Felder)
2 "Eruption," Van Halen (Edward Van Halen)
3 "Comfortably Numb," Pink Floyd (David Gilmour)
4 "Crossroads," Cream (Eric Clapton)
5 "Voodoo Chile," The Jimi Hendrix Experience (Jimi Hendrix)
6 "Parisienne Walkways," Gary Moore
7 "All Right Now," Free (Paul Kossoff)
8 "Since I've Been Loving You," Led Zeppelin (Jimmy Page)
9 "Bohemian Rhapsody," Queen (Brian May)
10 "Sultans of Swing," Dire Straits (Mark Knopfler)
11 "All Along the Watchtower," The Jimi Hendrix Experience (Jimi Hendrix)
12 "Shine on You Crazy Diamond," Pink Floyd (David Gilmour)
13 "Stairway to Heaven," Led Zeppelin (Jimmy Page)
14 "For the Love of God," Steve Vai
15 "Still in Love with You," Thin Lizzy (Gary Moore)
16 "Child in Time, Deep Purple" (Ritchie Blackmore)
17 "Still Got the Blues (For You)," Gary Moore

Continued on p.100

PRS CUSTOM 24

1975

In early 1975 Paul Reed Smith noticed that guitarists were using Gibsons for solos and Fenders for rhythm, so he decided to build a guitar suited to both functions. The result was ¼ inch (6 mm) longer than a Gibson and ½ inch (13 mm) shorter than a Fender. The guitar was slimmer than a Les Paul, but built from mahogany and curly maple like a Gibson with the horns of a Fender. The vibrato bar is an update of the Stratocaster's and its five-way pickup selector includes coil-tap positions that produce both Gibson- and Fender-like tones. It comes in a huge array of finishes and the rosewood fingerboard can be inlaid with PRS trademark birds in flight in abalone.

The intonation screws on the saddle adjust the length of the string to ensure pitch accuracy.

A 2005 20th Anniversary PRS Custom 24

Locking tuners

Rosewood fingerboard

PRS bird inlays

Glued-in mahogany neck

Hybrid Theory by Linkin Park

Famous players

★ Carlos Santana

★ Al Di Meola

★ Nils Lofgren

★ Alex Lifeson of Rush

★ Mike Oldfield

★ Mike Shinoda of Linkin Park

★ Dave Navarro of Jane's Addiction

Twin PRS pickups

Floating PRS vibrato with Teflon nut

Five-way rotary selector

Solid mahogany body with carved maple top

Tone and volume controls

20th

Although dots are available, the abalone bird inlays add individuality to the design.

Top 100 Guitar Solos, continued from p.97

Continued on p.101

A silkworm moth and a cocoon

I've been wrapped in silky sounds!

A classical tale

Until World War II classical guitars used gut for the treble stings with metal wound round floss silk cores for the bass. But gut strings were difficult to make true and regular, particularly in the higher registers. They got out of tune easily and frayed on the frets. And silk floss broke easily, so bass strings had to be built heavily to take the strain, inhibiting their sustain.

DECALOMANIA

"Decalomania" swept the United States in the 1920s and 1930s when guitar tops were covered in fancy decals.

Continued from p.100

Continued on p.102

The P-90 Pickup

After World War II, Gibson abandoned the bulky Charlie Christian pickup for the smaller P-60. It was a single-coil unit designed to be fitted into, rather than on top of, the guitar. Clamped in place by two screws, one at each end of the plastic casing, it could not be raised or lowered to adjust the distance of the strings. Guitars equipped with the P-90 came with both volume and tone control. The P-90 provided the sound of the Gibson until the mid 1950s.

> *Where did the birds come from? My mother was a bird-watcher; I grabbed a bird-watching guide and stole the pictures out of it.*

PAUL REED SMITH ON THE ABALONE BIRD INLAYS ON HIS GUITARS

*Top 100 Guitar Solos, continued
from p.101*

58 "And Your Bird Can Sing," The
Beatles (George Harrison)
59 "Green Tinted Sixties Mind,"
Mr. Big (Paul Gilbert)
60 "These Are the Days of Our
Lives," Queen (Brian May)
61 "Yo Mama," Frank Zappa
62 "Rocky Mountain Way,"
Joe Walsh
63 "Paranoid Android," Radiohead
(Johnny Greenwood)
64 "Something," The Beatles
(George Harrison)
65 "Dry County," Bon Jovi
(Ritchie Sambora)
66 "Surfing with the Alien,"
Joe Satriani
67 "Mr. Crowley," Ozzy Osborne
(Randy Rhoads)
68 "Jump," Van Halen
(Edward Van Halen)
69 "Love In An Elevator,"
Aerosmith (Joe Perry)
70 "Light My Fire," Jose Feliciano
71 "Alive," Pearl Jam
(Mark Mccready)
72 "The Loner," Gary Moore
73 "Kid Charlemagne," Steely Dan
(Larry Carlton)
74 "Summer Song," Joe Satriani
75 "Big Trouble," David Lee Roth
(Steve Vai)
76 "Resurrection," Brian May
77 "While My Guitar Gently
Weeps," The Beatles (Eric
Clapton and George Harrison)
78 "I Want It All," Queen
(Brian May)
79 "Stargazer," Rainbow
(Ritchie Blackmore)

Continued on p.103

Sample of written vihuela music
by the Spanish composer Miguel
de Fuenllana (c.1500–79)

GUITAR MUSIC ON PAPER

Early guitar music was written down in the
form of a tablature, showing the fingering of
the frets rather that the notes to be played.
Horizontal lines represented the strings. The
top line in the French and Italian system
represented the treble string, the reasoning
being that it was the highest in pitch. The
Spanish, however, used the bottom line to
represent the treble string on the grounds that
it was, physically, closer to the ground. To
confuse matters further the Italians and
Spanish used numbers to specify which frets
were to be fingered, while the French used
letters. The rhythm was indicated above the
stave, while the length of time the note should
be held was left up to the player.

Continued from p.102

80 "Sunshine of Your Love," Cream (Eric Clapton)
81 "Rough Boy," ZZ Top (Billy Gibbons)
82 "Road To Hell, Part 2," Chris Rea
83 "Tubular Bells," Mike Oldfield
84 "Paranoid," Black Sabbath (Tony Iommi)
85 "Foxy Lady," The Jimi Hendrix Experience (Jimi Hendrix)
86 "The Forgotten: Part 1," Joe Satriani
87 "Lazy," Deep Purple (Ritchie Blackmore)
88 "The Supernatural," John Mayall's Bluesbreakers (Peter Green)
89 "Bold as Love," The Jimi Hendrix Experience (Jimi Hendrix)
90 "Mother Knows Best," Richard Thompson
91 "Cry for the Nations," The Michael Schenker Group
92 "He Man Woman Hater," Extreme (Nuno Bettencourt)
93 "Samba Pa Ti," Santana (Carlos Santana)
94 "No-One Said It Would Be Easy," Sheryl Crow (David Baerwald)
95 "Echoes, Pink Floyd" (David Gilmour)
96 "She's Not There," Santana (Carlos Santana)
97 "I Am the Resurrection," Stone Roses (John Squire)
98 "Song 2," Blur (Graham Coxon)
99 "You Love Us," Manic Street Preachers (James Dean Bradfield)
100 "A Kinder Eye," Allan Holdsworth

Blues guitarist and singer Arthur "Blind" Blake c.1927

Blind Blake

The guitarist Blind Blake was one of the first African-American recording stars, but little is known of him. He signed for Paramount in 1926 and recorded eight tracks with the label, including several hits. Then he simply disappeared. No one is even sure what his real name was. He signed his contracts "Arthur Blake," but it is thought that his real name was Phelps.

66 **I made my first guitar. I made it out of a cigar box and a good stout long board, and it had five strings of baling wire. Hurt my fingers on it. That was when I was just a farm boy.** 99

ROBERT PETE WILLIAMS

BURNS MARVIN

1964

Hank Marvin of The Shadows was, famously, the first guitarist in the U.K. to have a Stratocaster. "It was a flamingo pink one," he said. "Cliff [Richard] ordered it from the Fender catalogue." The band's Bruce Welch also had one, while the bassist Jet Harris had a Fender P-Bass. However, Welch found problems with the tuning of his Stratocaster and turned to British guitar maker James Burns. He came up with the Marvin, which disguised the Fender body shape with mock-tortoiseshell plates. Marvin himself came up with a violin-style scroll on the headstock. Burns went through 30 prototypes in two years until he came up with what Marvin called "the perfect guitar." The instrument can be heard on The Shadows' "The Rise and Fall of Flingel Bunt."

1964 Burns Marvin

Rosewood
fingerboard

Bolt-on
maple neck

Multiple
jigsaw
tortoiseshell
body plates
(newer
models in
mint green)

Three
Rez-O-Matic
single-coil
pickups with
alnico
magnets

Solid
American
alder body

Rez-O-Tube
vibrato
system

Jim Burns and
Hank Marvin

Famous players

☆ Hank Marvin and Bruce
Welch of The Shadows

When Hank Marvin's
Burns Marvin was stolen
in 1970, he returned to
playing Fender guitars.

The Pizzar

In 1998 New York guitar maker Robert Benedetto created the solid-body "Pizzar," which was exhibited at the National Association of Music Merchants show in Los Angeles, California, in 1999. It was shaped like a slice of New York-style pizza with real oregano, garlic, and other herbs and spices sealed in with lacquer. Otherwise it had a regular spec:

- ✪ Basswood body
- ✪ Width of neck at nut—1¾ inches (4.5 cm)
- ✪ Mahogany neck
- ✪ Two Kent Armstrong pickups
- ✪ Burgundy finish on back, sides, and neck
- ✪ Two black strap buttons.

> **The technique and feeling of playing pop is instinctive in the same way that it is in the blues...**
>
> JOHN WILLIAMS

Fernando Sor and his guitar

ON A KNIFE EDGE

The blues composer and musician W.C. Handy (1873–1958) was traveling in Mississippi in 1903 when he heard a new sound: "One night at Tutwiler, as I nodded in the railroad station while waiting for a train that had been delayed nine hours, life suddenly took me by the shoulder and wakened me with a start. A lean, loose-jointed Negro had commenced plunking a guitar beside me while I slept. His clothes were rags; his feet peeped out of his shoes. His face had on it some of the sadness of the ages. As he played, he pressed a knife on the strings of the guitar in a manner popularized by Hawaiian guitarists who used steel bars. The effect was unforgettable... the weirdest music I ever heard."

ROLL OVER BEETHOVEN

Born in Barcelona, the child prodigy Fernando Sor (1778–1839) was a guitarist and composer who toured Europe, wowing audiences in London, Paris, Berlin, Warsaw, and Moscow, where he composed a funeral march for the Tsar. He died in France where he was known as "the Beethoven of the guitar"—though others called Beethoven "the Sor of the piano." Beethoven is thought to have stolen the theme for the Moonlight Sonata from Sor.

Railroad station on the Mississippi River in 1907

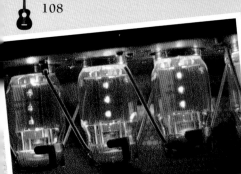

KT88 power tubes in a
Traynor YBA200 amplifier

The birth of feedback

With rock 'n' roll, purity of sound
went out of the window. Distortion
and feedback became an important
element. Recalling his early days with
The Yardbirds, Jeff Beck said: "Playing
in all those small clubs you always get
feedback because of the bad systems,
and really the electrical thing hadn't
been sewn up. All the amps were
underpowered and screwed up to full
volume, and always whistling. My
amp was always whistling! And I'd
kick it and bash it and a couple of
tubes would break, and I was playing
largely on an amp with just one
output valve still working. It would
feed back, so I decided to use it rather
than fight it. It was hopeless to try and
play a chord, because it would just
rrrr, so when I progressed on to a
bigger amp and I didn't get it, I kinda
missed it. I went to hit a note and
there wasn't any distortion; too clean.
It was horrible. So the ideal thing was
to get the beauty of the feedback, but
controllable feedback."

GREATEST BLUES GUITARISTS

This list, compiled by the website
digitaldreamdoor.com, ranks guitarists who
have "exhibited a clear 'Blues' thread
throughout their careers:"

1 T-Bone Walker
2 B.B. King
3 Stevie Ray Vaughan
4 Robert Johnson
5 Albert King
6 Eric Clapton
7 Buddy Guy
8 Mike Bloomfield
9 Peter Green
10 Johnny Winter
11 Otis Rush
12 Muddy Waters
13 Ronnie Earl
14 Freddie King
15 Earl Hooker
16 Elmore James
17 Albert Collins
18 Hubert Sumlin
19 Duane Allman
20 John Lee Hooker

JUDAS GOES ELECTRIC

Bob Dylan, the acoustic guitar hero of
the early 1960s, was dubbed "Judas" in
England when he went electric in 1965.

I'll show you how to play flamenco!

Railroad learning

Country guitar pioneer Sam McGee (1894–1975) learned his fingerpicking style from African-American bluesmen. Guitars were rare in the Tennessee hills before World War I, but McGee was determined to learn. Then the family moved into town. "My daddy ran a little store, and these section hands would come over from the railroad at noon," said McGee. "Well, after they finished their lunch, they would play guitars… that's where I learned to love the blues tunes. Black people were about the only people that played the guitar then." Jimmie Rodgers (1897–1933)—the "Singing Brakeman"—also learnt to play the guitar from African-Americans working on the railroad.

Flamboyant flamenco

In Seville, Spain, in the 19th century flamenco guitarists would try and outdo each other by outrageous acts of showmanship. They would play with a glove on one hand, or with the guitar held above their head.

DANELECTRO SHORTHORN

1956

Danelectro, the company founded in 1947 by Nathan Daniel, originally made mail-order Silvertone guitars for Sears Roebuck. He also made guitars under the Danelectro name for the budget market. He had figured that students wanted an instrument that was pretty disposable. So he stapled together a poplar frame and covered it in Masonite (a type of hardboard). He stuck some vinyl around the join and added pickups made from lipstick tubes. It was cheap. But it did not fall to pieces—and it sounded good. The Danelectro Standard became the Shorthorn. Jimmy Page bought one when he was with The Yardbirds. It can be heard on live versions of Led Zeppelin's "Kashmir," "Babe I'm Gonna Leave You," and "Black Mountain Side."

A bass version of the Longhorn model was played by John Entwhistle on "My Generation."

1956 Danelectro Shorthorn

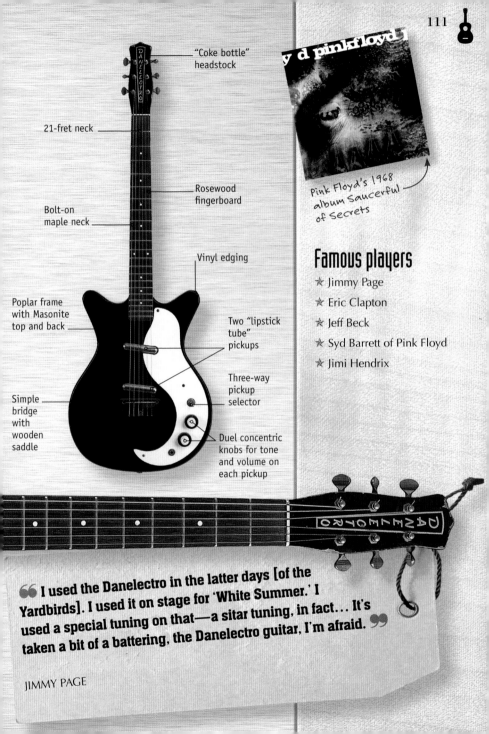

111

"Coke bottle" headstock

21-fret neck

Rosewood fingerboard

Bolt-on maple neck

Vinyl edging

Poplar frame with Masonite top and back

Two "lipstick tube" pickups

Three-way pickup selector

Simple bridge with wooden saddle

Duel concentric knobs for tone and volume on each pickup

Pink Floyd's 1968 album Saucerful of Secrets

Famous players

* Jimmy Page
* Eric Clapton
* Jeff Beck
* Syd Barrett of Pink Floyd
* Jimi Hendrix

66 **I used the Danelectro in the latter days [of the Yardbirds]. I used it on stage for 'White Summer.' I used a special tuning on that—a sitar tuning, in fact... It's taken a bit of a battering, the Danelectro guitar, I'm afraid.** 99

JIMMY PAGE

Paul Reed Smith
PRS Singlecut

Weight loss

Some otherwise solid-bodied guitars, such as the Paul Reed Smith PRS Singlecut or Gibson Les Paul, had "weight relief" holes drilled in the body to make them lighter. This affected the sound. So the Les Paul Supreme edition is now described as "chambered" as it is claimed that these weight-relief holes have a positive effect on the acoustics.

66 Just look at what my invention hath wrought on humankind! A lot of fathers and mothers probably would like to kill me... Then again, if it hadn't been me, it would have been someone else. 99

PAUL TUTMARC, PIONEER OF THE ELECTRIC GUITAR

ACOUSTIC GUITAR STRING GAUGES

Name	1	2	3	4	5	6
	(E)	(B)	(G)	(D)	(A)	(E)
Extra light (10–47)	.010	.014	.023	.030	.039	.047
Custom light (11–52)	.011	.015	.023	.032	.042	.052
Light (12–54)	.012	.016	.025	.032	.042	.054
Light/Medium (12.5–55)	.0125	.0165	.0255	.0335	.0435	.055
Medium (13–56)	.013	.017	.026	.035	.045	.056

Strings .023-inches in diameter and above are bronze wound.

ELECTRIC GUITAR STRING GAUGES

Name	1	2	3	4	5	6
	(E)	(B)	(G)	(D)	(A)	(E)
Extra super light (8–38)	.008	.010	.015	.021	.030	.038
Extra super light plus (8.5–39)	.0085	.0105	.015	.022	.032	.039
Super light (9–42)	.009	.011	.016	.024	.032	.042
Super light plus (9.5–44)	.0095	.0115	.016	.024	.034	.044
Regular light (10–46)	.010	.013	.017	.026	.036	.046
Extra light w/heavy bass (9–46)	.009	.013	.021	.029	.036	.046
Medium (11–48/49)	.011	.014	.018	.028	.038	.048/49
Light top/Heavy bottom (10–52)	.010	.013	.017	.032	.042	.052
Medium w/wound G string (11–52)	.011	.013	.020	.030	.042	.052
Heavy (12–54)	.012	.016	.020	.032	.042	.054
Extra heavy (13–56)	.013	.017	.026	.036	.046	.056

Standard string gauges are in inches (0.001 in = 0.0254 mm). The larger the diameter, the heavier the string is. Strings .021-inches in diameter and above are wound.

Oahu guitars

Based in Cleveland, Ohio, Oahu made guitars in the 1930s that boasted "new SafeTiString posts," a "special reinforced bridge," and the "Oahu deluxe hand-rubbed finish." The catalog continues: "For one who appreciates a neat looking instrument without elaborate handiwork and whose primary interest is tone quality and workmanship, we recommend this instrument as the best money can buy. It is guaranteed to last a lifetime." The extra-large jumbo guitar with a fancy decal cost a hefty $98.

BASS GUITAR STRING GAUGES

Name	1 (G)	2 (D)	3 (A)	4 (E)	5 (B)
Light or "soft" (40–100)	.040	.060	.080	.100	.125
Medium (45–105)	.045	.065	.085	.105	.130
Heavy (50–110)	.050	.075	.095	.110	.135

Bass guitar strings are sometimes made for a particular scale length and come in short, medium, long, and extra or super long.

BLIND WILLIE JOHNSON

Eric Clapton called Blind Willie Johnson's "It's Nobody's Fault But Mine" the finest slide playing ever recorded. Born in Marlin, Texas, around 1900, he was blinded when his stepmother threw dye in his face at the age of seven. He recorded between 1927 and 1930, but was forced to go back to playing on the streets during the Depression. He died when, after surviving a house fire, he returned home to sleep on a wet mattress and contracted pneumonia. He was refused admission to hospital because he was black. However, his death certificate says he died of malaria, with syphilis as a contributing factor.

Daddy made it

Back in the early 1960s, the teenage Brian May couldn't afford to buy an electric guitar. So his father Harold, who was an electronics draftsman, stepped up to the challenge.

There were no spare parts for Gibsons or Fenders in England in those days, so he had to improvise. He made the body from blockboard with mahogany veneer, the fingerboard from oak, and he used mahogany taken from the surround of a 200-year-old fireplace to make the neck. Harold then stained the body red and painted the fingerboard black. He used pearl buttons to make the dot markers on the fingerboard and finished the guitar by hand with a plastic coating.

The Mays made their own pickups and the homemade knife-edge tremolo used a motorcycle spring to counter the tension of the strings and bring them back into pitch. A knitting needle was commandeered to make the vibrato arm.

The output was then fed to a homemade transistor amplifier built into a bookshelf hi-fi speaker by Queen bassist John Deacon. In performance, the sound is boosted through a modified Vox AC30 amplifier with treble booster.

Recently, May has had his Red Special—sometimes known as the Fireplace Guitar—restored by Australian maker Greg Fryer. But May has given another maker, Andrew Guyton of Norfolk, England, permission to make a limited quantity of these guitars for sale. The original cost just £18 ($30) to build.

An Andrew Guyton
Red Special

66 *I'm quite stunned that it's lasted this long really, but nothing else has quite come up to it for that warm, sustaining sound. A combination of design and luck I suppose.* **99**

BRIAN MAY ON HIS HOMEMADE
RED SPECIAL

DUESENBERG STARPLAYER TV

1995

German luthier Dieter Gölsdorf started making kit guitars under the name Rockinger. Then he developed a fine-tuning vibrato system called the Rockinger Tru Tune and his own version of the Gibson P-90 pickup. In 1986 he came up with a series of futuristic designs. Then, in the mid-1990s, he reverted to a retro style, including the solid-bodied Starplayer Special and the semi-solid Starplayer TV with a Gibson 335-style solid center block and a single f-hole. He gave them weird and wonderful finishes—blue sparkle, green pearl, black crocodile-style vinyl—which made them look good on video. And the combination of Duesenberg DP-90 and Grand Vintage pickups means that it can switch from blues to rock, taking in funk if you leave both pickups on.

Duesenberg
Starplayer TV

Rosewood fingerboards

Glued maple neck

Laminated maple body

Duensenberg DP-90 pickup

Grand Vintage pickup

Art Deco-style scratchplate

Three-way pickup selector switch

Single f-hole

Master tone and volume controls

Super Tremolo vibrato

The Very Best of Elvis Costello

THE VERY BEST OF elvis costello

Famous players

✶ Elvis Costello
✶ Ronnie Wood
✶ ZZ Top
✶ Davey Johnstone of the Elton John band
✶ Mike McCready of Pearl Jam
✶ Mike Campbell

Ronnie Wood signature model Duesenberg Starplayer

PICK A PIKASSO

In 1984 Pat Metheny went to Manzer Guitars and asked them to build him a guitar with "as many strings as possible." The result was the Pikasso, which has two sounds holes and four necks. It has a special wedge shape; the body is tapered so that the side closest to the player's upper body is thinner than the side that rests on the knee. This allows it to fit more comfortably under the player's arm and makes it easier to see the top of the guitar. Manzer have since made this option available on all their flat-top guitars. It has a state-of-the-art piezo pickup system, including a hexaphonic pickup on the six-string section that allowed Metheny to couple it to his Syclavier computer system so that it can be used as a synthesizer or to trigger sampled sounds. The Pikasso weighs 14¾ pounds (6.7 kg) and can be mounted on a stand. When 42 strings are tuned to concert pitch, the instrument is under some 1,000 pounds (450 kg) of pressure.

SET-UPS OF THE STARS

Robben Ford

The smooth LA guitar tone of jazz fusion guitarist Robben Ford originated with a Gibson Super 400 arch-top played through a Fender Bassman. Later he used a Gibson ES-335, a signature Fender, and Baker guitars. His set-up passes the sound through wah-wah and volume pedals, a TC Electronic 2290 for chorus and delay, and a Lexicon PCM-70 for reverb to a Dumble amplifier.

GREATEST JAZZ GUITARISTS

The following list was compiled by www.digitaldreamdoor.com:

1 Wes Montgomery
2 Django Reinhardt
3 Pat Metheny
4 Joe Pass
5 Charlie Christian
6 John McLaughlin
7 Allan Holdsworth
8 Grant Green
9 John Scofield
10 Jim Hall
11 Larry Coryell
12 Kenny Burrell
13 Bill Frisell
14 Larry Carlton
15 Pat Martino
16 Mike Stern
17 Al Di Meola
18 Lenny Breau
19 Herb Ellis
20 John Abercrombie

> ❝ Sometimes you want to give up the guitar, you'll hate the guitar. But if you stick with it, you're gonna be rewarded. ❞

JIMI HENDRIX

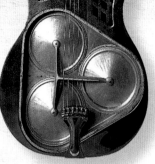

Tricone Sound

The body of National tricone guitars is made of German silver, also known as white brass or nickel silver. It is an alloy of around 65 percent copper, 20 per cent zinc, and 15 per cent nickel. The same material is often used to make fret wire. The resonator system comprises three aluminum cones, six inches (15 cm) in diameter and lathe-spun to a thickness of 0.005 inches (0.13 mm) and embossed with a radiating pattern of lines for strength. The centers of the three cones are connected by a T-shaped bridge bar with a maple insert that the strings rest on. The delicate cones are protected by a triangular cover plate.

National tricones have a sweeter, richer sound than later single-cone models, which sound more like a banjo. The sound is full of harmonics and has a faint but unmistakable reverb. A few blues players (such as Tampa Red, Black Ace, Memphis Minnie, and Peetie Wheatstraw) acquired tricones, but they were expensive and were usually the instrument of jazz, calypso, and Hawaiian players.

FENDER FACTS

Electronics-whiz Leo Fender (1909–91) ran his own radio repair shop in Fullerton, California, while selling and renting amplification equipment to musicians. During World War II he met Clayton Orr "Doc" Kauffman, an inventor and a lap steel guitar player, who had worked for Rickenbacker. Together they formed K&F Manufacturing, producing lap steel guitars with a pickup patented by Fender and an amplifier kit he had designed. In 1946 he broke away to form his own company in Fullerton, California. In April 1950, Fender produced the Fender Esquire, followed by the Broadcaster, which was renamed the Telecaster. This guitar had a solid body with a bolt-on neck, making it perfect for mass production. Fender's Precision Bass (P-Bass), the first mass-produced electric bass guitar, was released the following year.

1952 Fender Esquire

TWO-FINGER TECHNIQUE

The great French jazz guitarist Django Reinhardt (1910–53) played chords using just two fingers of his left hand. A gypsy, at the age of eighteen he was living in a caravan with his first wife, who made artificial flowers out of paper and celluloid. One night on the way to bed, he knocked over a candle. In the resulting fire, he was badly burned, leaving the third and fourth fingers paralyzed. Doctors told him that he would never play guitar again. Instead, he learned to play in a new way, revolutionizing jazz guitar techniques.

Django Reinhardt

Disraeli Gears by Cream

MAKING CREAM

In 1966 Eric Clapton got together with Jack Bruce on bass and Ginger Baker on drums to form a blues trio along the lines of Buddy Guy's group. Their aim was to play the blues to a small audience. But at their first gig, the Windsor Jazz and Blues Festival, they ran out of numbers and began to improvise. "So we just made up a twelve-bar blues," said Clapton, "and that became Cream." The blues-based supergroup was hugely successful but broke up two years later.

Largest guitar ensemble

The record for the world's largest guitar ensemble was an event organized by the Thanks Jimi Festival, in Wroclaw, Rynek, Poland, on May 1, 2009 when 6,346 guitarists turned out. The rock band Deep Purple took part in this record-breaking attempt.

50 HEAVIEST RIFFS OF ALL TIME

The following chronological list is adapted from one produced in May 1995 by the editorial staff of *Guitar* magazine:

1 "All Day and All of the Night," The Kinks
2 "Purple Haze," The Jimi Hendrix Experience
3 "Sunshine of your Love," Cream
4 "You Keep Me Hangin' On," Vanilla Fudge
5 "In-A-Gadda-Da-Vida," Iron Butterfly
6 "Born To Be Wild," Steppenwolf
7 "Whole Lotta Love," Led Zeppelin
8 "Moby Dick," Led Zeppelin
9 "Black Sabbath," Black Sabbath
10 "Mississippi Queen," Mountain
11 "Iron Man," Black Sabbath
12 "I'm Eighteen," Alice Cooper
13 "Situation," The Jeff Beck Group
14 "Smoke on the Water," Deep Purple
15 "Frankenstein," The Edgar Winter Group
16 "I Just Want to Make Love to You," Foghat
17 "Train Kept a-Rollin'," Aerosmith
18 "Man on the Silver Mountain," Rainbow
19 "Stranglehold," Ted Nugent
20 "The Temples of Syrinx from 2112," Rush
21 "Jailbreak," Thin Lizzy
22 "God of Thunder," Kiss
23 "Crazy on You," Heart
24 "Godzilla," Blue Oyster Cult

Continued on p.124

G&L ASAT

1979

After leaving Music Man, Leo Fender set up G&L with George Fullerton in Fender Avenue, Fullerton, California. They came up with the ASAT guitar, a design that harked back to Fender's glory days with the Telecaster and Stratocaster. But Fender had moved on. He devised the Magnetic Field Design pickup with soft-iron pole pieces whose height could be adjusted, allowing the musician to set the output of each individual string. It also had an improved saddle-lock bridge that reduced the side-to-side movement of the strings and prevented loss of sustain. The later

Rampage model had a simplified S-design with one humbucker pickup and a Kahler vibrato system. This did not prove so popular and was discontinued in 1991.

MAGNETIC FIELD DESIGN PICKUP

Strings

Height adjustable pole pieces mean the closer to the string the greater the output

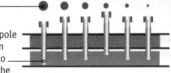

1989 G&L ASAT

Six-a-side head

Glued-on rosewood or maple fingerboard

Two-piece maple neck

Solid alder or ash body

Two single-coil magnetic field design pickups

Simple three-saddle bridge

Three-way selector switch

Tone and volume controls

Iris DeMent's album *Infamous Angel*

Famous players

★ Andrew and Tim Farris of INXS

★ Art Alexakis of Everclear

★ Iris DeMent

★ Deano Brown of The Tim McGraw Band

★ Probyn Gregory of The Brian Wilson Band

★ Jerry Cantrell of Alice in Chains

JUST LIKE THE OLD DAYS

When Leo Fender set up G&L with George Fullerton in 1979, they wanted to make guitars "just like in the old days." He quickly came up with the ASAT, which he said stood for "Another Strat, Another Tele."

50 Heaviest Riffs of All Time.
continued from p.121

Tremolux amplifier

Tremolo or vibrato?

The tremolo arm on a guitar actually produces vibrato—that is, a rapid variation in pitch. The misnomer is attributed to Leo Fender who introduced the Vibroverb amplifier in 1963. This actually produced a tremolo effect—that is, a rapid variation in volume. Ten years earlier, Fender had introduced the Tremolux amplifier, which used the musical terminology correctly.

OFF THE WALL

Robert Johnson recorded the tracks that appear on his influential 1961 album *King of the Delta Blues Singers* in hotel rooms in Dallas, Texas, in 1936 and 1937. During the recording sessions, he turned his back on the recording engineer. The myth circulated that he did this to hide his playing technique. It is more likely that he was using an effect called "corner loading"—playing his guitar straight at the wall to increase the immediacy and mid-range sound.

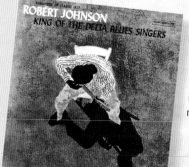

The electric harp-guitar

The harp-guitar may seem like an anachronistic throwback, but in the 1990s it went electric—twice. Masahiko "Masaki" Ohno of the Japanese noise band Solmania built his own electric harp guitar. The band specialized in guitars with strange body shapes, extra necks, strings and pickups in unusual places, and extraneous gadgetry. And the experimental Dutch guitar maker Yuri Landman made a 17-string electric harp-guitar for Finn Andrews of the London-based Indie band The Veils.

Guitar made by Yuri Landman for Finn Andrews of The Veils

THE VICTORIANS UNPLUGGED

In 1862 the Spanish guitarist Julián Arcas played at the London home of the Duke of Wellington. He was enthusiastically received by Queen Victoria's daughter, the Duchess of Cambridgeshire, who put on two more concerts for him at the Brighton Pavilion. Another two daughters of Queen Victoria, Princess Louise and Princess Beatrice, were taught to play the guitar by Catherine Pelzer, a child prodigy who styled herself Madame Sidney Pratten.

Queen Victoria with her extended family

Muddy Waters
c. 1979

Waters goes electric

Muddy Waters (1913–83) played the acoustic guitar in Mississippi juke joints where he came into contact with the likes of Son House and Robert Nighthawk. It was only when he moved to Chicago in 1943 that he acquired his first electric guitar—a gift from his uncle. "I was playing the clubs," he said. "And you can't hear an acoustic in a liquor club. There's just too much noise."

EIGHT STRINGS FOR METAL

Eight-string guitars are used by metal bands such as GWAR, Ihsahn, Meshuggah, After the Burial, Rusty Cooley, Wayde Cooper, Animals as Leaders, Whitechapel, Scale the Summit, Deftones, Stations, the Acacia Strain, High on Fire, Trapt, Ad Ruinas, the Freelancers, Clockwork, and Dino Cazares of Asesino, Fear Factory, and Divine Heresy. Even the pop-rock band Triumphant Return has been seen using eight-string guitars. Small manufacturers such as the U.K.'s Blackmachine, Switzerland's Hufschmid, Oni, and Mike Sherman make eight-string models, and even Japanese giant Ibanez now produces an eight-stringer.

Flat-top guitar

Arch-top guitar

Flat-top versus arch-top

On the flat-top guitar, the strings end at the bridge, which is glued to the soundboard, so the vibration of the strings is transmitted to the table by the horizontal rocking of the bridge. On an arch-top guitar, the strings are stretched over the bridge and terminate at a tailpiece, so string vibration is transmitted to the table by the vertical movement of the bridge.

THE WORLD'S GREATEST AIR GUITARISTS

The winners of the Air Guitar World Championships are:

1996	Oikku Yinen (Finland)
1997	Ville Paakkari (Finland)
1998	Juha Hippi (Finland)
1999	Johanna Ala-Siurua (Finland)
2000	Markus Vainionpää (Finland)
2001	Zac "Mr. Magnet" Monro (U.K.)
2002	Zac "Mr. Magnet" Monro (U.K.)
2003	David "C-Diddy" Jung (U.S.A.)
2004	Tarquin "The Tarkness" Keys (New Zealand)
2005	Michael "The Destroyer" Heffels (Netherlands)
2006	Ochi "Dainoji" Yosuke (Japan)
2007	Ochi "Dainoji" Yosuke (Japan)
2008	Craig "Hot Lixx Hulahan" Billmeier (U.S.A.)
2009	Sylvain "Gunther Love" Quimene (France)
2010	Sylvain "Gunther Love" Quimene (France)

Kevin "Narvalwaker" Leloux at the 2010 Air Guitar World Championships in Oulu, Finland

HAMER STANDARD

1974

In 1973 Paul Hamer and Jol Dantzig started a shop in Chicago, where they renovated old guitars. They then began building guitars of their own. The Standard was the first model they produced and was based on Gibson's angular Explorer, but also borrowed features from the Les Paul. Although the ideas man was Dantzig, they used the name Hamer because it sounded more "rock-and-roll." The Standard proved popular with musicians, who had become increasingly discontented with modern Gibsons, but did not want to fork out for vintage guitars. Hamer then followed up with the more conventionally shaped Sunburst.

1979 Hamer Sunburst

Hamer Standard

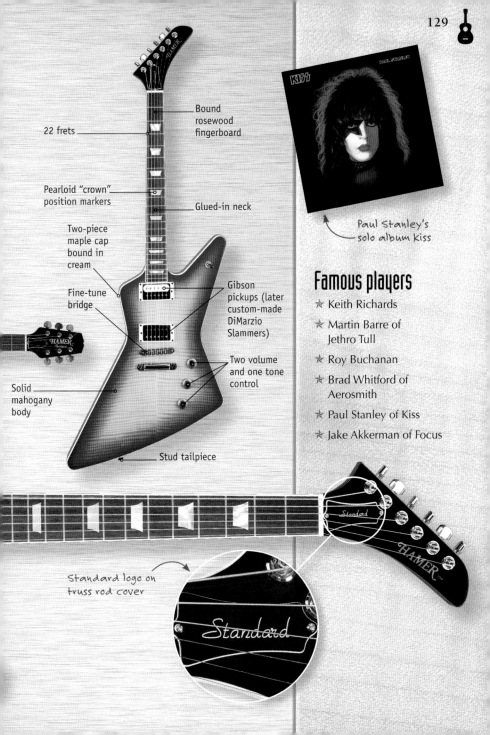

Bound
rosewood
fingerboard

22 frets

Pearloid "crown"
position markers

Glued-in neck

Two-piece
maple cap
bound in
cream

Gibson
pickups (later
custom-made
DiMarzio
Slammers)

Fine-tune
bridge

Two volume
and one tone
control

Solid
mahogany
body

Stud tailpiece

Paul Stanley's
solo album Kiss

Famous players

✴ Keith Richards
✴ Martin Barre of
  Jethro Tull
✴ Roy Buchanan
✴ Brad Whitford of
  Aerosmith
✴ Paul Stanley of Kiss
✴ Jake Akkerman of Focus

Standard logo on
truss rod cover

Standard

IN THE MOOD

The Moodswinger is a guitar-shaped 12-stringed electric zither built by Yuri Landman in 2006 for the New York dance-punk band The Liars. It also has three bridges. A copy can now be seen in the Musical Instrument Museum in Phoenix, Arizona. Landman also created a version called the Home Swinger for workshops at festivals, where participants make their own in four hours. In 2010 workshops were held in the Knitting Factory in Brooklyn, New York, and the Eyedrum arts center in Atlanta, Georgia.

GREATEST AVANT GARDE GUITARISTS

The following is adapted from a list compiled by www.digitaldreamdoor.com:

1 Derek Bailey
2 Fred Frith
3 Henry Kaiser
4 Eugene Chadbourne
5 James Blood Ulmer
6 Sonny Sharrok
7 Glenn Branca
8 Sonny Greenwich
9 Bill Frisell
10 Mark Ribot
11 Rene Lussier
12 Keiji Haino
13 Pierre Dorge
14 Nels Cline
15 Loren MazzaCane Connors
16 Rauol Bjorkenheim
17 Elliot Sharp
18 Joe Morris
19 Hans Reichel
20 Marc Ducret

I'm training to be a classical guitarist.

NAIL BITING

Andrés Segovia developed the technique of relaxing his right hand and striking the strings with the left side of his fingernails. Others favor using the right side of the nails.

Abstract challenge

Abstract Guitars of Las Vegas give a promise to their customers: "If you can dream it, Abstract can build it." They have 45 different types of wood: 12 for the fingerboard alone—and 50 headstock designs that can angle and tilt. You can have 22, 24, 27, 33, or 36 frets; you are invited to pick your own fret size in nickel, stainless steel, or gold-tone adamantium. You can have any type of pickup, spring-loaded or hard-mounted, and any type of bridge. And you can choose you own name.

Longest guitar concert

The world record for the longest concert by multiple artists was set at the Balatonfüred Guitar Festival, Hungary, in 2008, when 350 groups played continuously for 216 hours. Classical, jazz, flamenco, and rock guitarists took to the stage for nine days, day and night. The youngest participant was only seven years old. The Hungarians had set the record at 192 hours in 2007, but that was then topped by the Canadians who stopped after 200 hours.

Albert Lee playing an Ernie Ball Music Man Albert Lee guitar in 2007

66 Sterling Ball (of Music Man) said to me one day, 'I think I have a guitar with your name on it'… I've been using the model ever since. 99

ALBERT LEE

TAKE YOUR PICK

There are many types of pick:

✪ **Standard plastic**: Available in a wide range of thicknesses to suit all styles. Many are available with a high-grip surface at the base of the pick.

✪ **Teardrop**: Smaller in size than the standard pick so can be tricky to use. Thicker gauges are favored by jazz guitarists.

✪ **Stainless steel**: Popular with rock guitarists, often chosen for its brash sound and attack. The downside is it can shorten string life and even damage the finish of your guitar.

✪ **Sharkfin**: So called because of its unusual shape. Both the smooth and serrated edge of the pick can be used to strike the strings.

✪ **Equal-sided**: Available in a range of sizes and thicknesses, any corner can be used to hit the strings.

TRICHET

Dirty dancing

The French musicologist Pierre Trichet (1586–1644) complained about the dancing that the guitar provoked—"even in France one finds courtesans and ladies who turn themselves into Spanish monkeys... Still there are some in our nation who leave everything behind in order to take up and study the guitar... is it because it has a certain something which is feminine and pleasing to women, flattering their hearts and making them inclined to voluptuousness?" he wonders.

> ❝ My first Telecaster was stolen, so I had to get a new one. The good thing about getting new equipment is that it comes from the shop and is not worn out after forty or fifty years of practice. ❞
>
> JONNY GREENWOOD

THE 100 GREATEST ROCK BASS GUITARISTS

The following list was compiled by www.digitaldreamdoor.com:

1 James Jamerson (Funk Brothers, session man)
2 John Entwistle (The Who)
3 Larry Graham (Sly & The Family Stone)
4 Chris Squire (Yes)
5 Jack Bruce (Cream)
6 Tony Levin (King Crimson, session man)
7 Geddy Lee (Rush)
8 Paul McCartney (The Beatles)
9 Louis Johnson (Brothers Johnson, session man)
10 Anthony Jackson (session man)
11 Flea (Red Hot Chili Peppers)
12 Marcus Miller (session man)
13 Les Claypool (Primus)
14 Chuck Rainey (session man)
15 Billy Sheehan (Niacin, Mr. Big, Steve Vai)
16 Geezer Butler (Black Sabbath)
17 Will Lee (session man)
18 Michael Manring (Attention Deficit, session man)
19 Nathan East (Eric Clapton, session man)
20 Rocco Prestia (Tower of Power)
21 John Paul Jones (Led Zeppelin)
22 Abe Laboriel (session man)
23 Stuart Hamm (Joe Satriani)
24 Donald "Duck" Dunn (The MGs)
25 Dave LaRue (Dixie Dregs)
26 Bob Babbitt (Funk Brothers, session man)

Continued on p.136

ZEMAITIS METAL FRONT

1971

British-born cabinet-maker and musician Tony Zemaitis started making guitars as a hobby, only to discover that there was an enthusiastic market for his products. In 1960 he became a full-time guitar maker. Ten years later he began experimenting with metal shields on the top of the guitar to prevent microphone noise being picked up by the guitar's pickups. Tony McPhee was the first top player to buy a Zemaitis guitar. After Ronnie Wood bought one, Keith Richards, Eric Clapton, and Ronnie Lane followed suit. He commissioned an engraver to engrave intricate patterns on the front. Then he began inlaying the front of his guitars with abalone and pearl. Both the metal and pearl-front guitars were custom made and changed hands for enormous prices.

Intricate engraved designs on the front

Zemaitis GZMF300

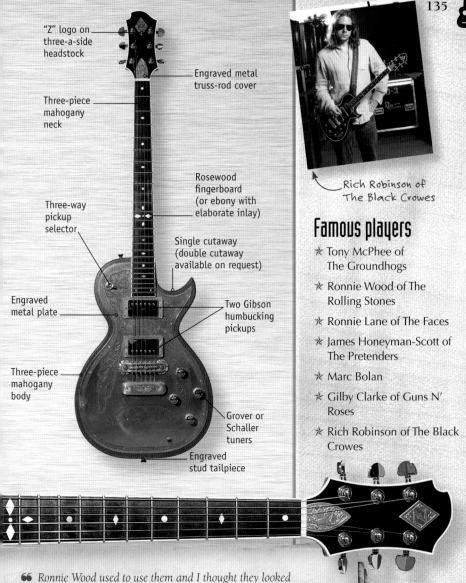

"Z" logo on three-a-side headstock

Engraved metal truss-rod cover

Three-piece mahogany neck

Rosewood fingerboard (or ebony with elaborate inlay)

Three-way pickup selector

Single cutaway (double cutaway available on request)

Engraved metal plate

Two Gibson humbucking pickups

Three-piece mahogany body

Grover or Schaller tuners

Engraved stud tailpiece

Rich Robinson of The Black Crowes

Famous players

* Tony McPhee of The Groundhogs

* Ronnie Wood of The Rolling Stones

* Ronnie Lane of The Faces

* James Honeyman-Scott of The Pretenders

* Marc Bolan

* Gilby Clarke of Guns N' Roses

* Rich Robinson of The Black Crowes

66 *Ronnie Wood used to use them and I thought they looked beautiful. I have two made of engraved metal with Gibson humbuckers and ebony fingerboards. One is a 22-fret guitar; the other a 24-fret. I've also got another 24-fret one, but the front is crushed mother-of-pearl. A Zemaitis definitely makes me play a bit more like Ron Wood.* 99

JAMES HONEYMAN-SCOTT OF THE PRETENDERS

The 100 Greatest Rock Bass Guitarists. continued from p.133

27 Phil Lesh (Grateful Dead)
28 Steve Harris (Iron Maiden)
29 Jack Casady (Jefferson Airplane, Hot Tuna)
30 Cliff Lee Burton (Metallica)
31 John Myung (Dream Theater)
32 John Deacon (Queen)
33 Willie Weeks (session man)
34 Carol Kaye (session woman)
35 Aston "Family Man" Barrett (Bob Marley & The Wailers)
36 Verdine White (Earth, Wind & Fire)
37 David Hungate (Toto, session man)
38 Robert "Kool" Bell (Kool & The Gang)
39 Joe Osborne (session man)
40 Phil Chen (Rod Stewart, session man)
41 Oteil Burbridge (Allman Brothers Band)
42 Freddie Washington (session man)
43 Nathan Watts (session man)
44 Louis Satterfield (Earth Wind & Fire, session man)
45 Andy West (Dixie Dregs)
46 Bootsy Collins (Funkadelic)
47 John Wetton (King Crimson)
48 Greg Lake (ELP)
49 Tim Bogert (Vanilla Fudge)
50 Mark King (Level 42)
51 Mike Watt (Minutemen)
52 Bernard Odum (James Brown, session man)
53 George Porter Jr. (Meters, session man)
54 Mike Gordon (Phish)
55 Bernard Edwards (Chic)

Continued on p.137

CHILD PRODIGY

Born in Córdoba, Spain, in 1942, renowned flamenco guitarist Paco Peña began taking guitar lessons from his brothers at the age of six. By the time he was twelve, he was appearing professionally on the concert stage. In 1985 he became the world's first professor of flamenco at the Rotterdam Conservatory and in 1997 he was awarded the Cross of the Order of Merit by the King of Spain.

Maker's mark

The Gibson logo first appeared on their headstocks in 1908. On the original headstock the peghead was inlaid with a moon and crescent motif.

OUTDATED!

In 1933, when folklorist John Lomax tracked down Huddie Ledbetter, better known as Leadbelly, in Angola jail, he found that he had a repertoire of around 500 songs. Lomax secured his parole a year later, and Leadbelly went north where he became the darling of college kids and the Greenwich Village set. However, when Lomax arranged a concert for him in Harlem's Apollo theater, African-Americans were not impressed, considering his music to be ten years out of date. Nevertheless, his New York home attracted folk and blues artists both black and white—including Woodie Guthrie, Sonny Terry, and Brownie McGhee. The songs he wrote, or adapted, such as "Rock Island Line," "Pick a Bale of Cotton," and "C.C. Rider," became key to the nascent folk revival. Leadbelly died in 1949.

Leadbelly strumming a 12-string guitar

Continued from p.136

56 Ryan Martinie (Mudvayne)
57 Willie Dixon (session man)
58 Andy Fraser (Free)
59 Trey Gunn (King Crimson)
60 Dave Schools (Widespread Panic)
61 Berry Oakley (Allman Brothers Band)
62 Jerry Jemmott (session man)
63 Roger Glover (Deep Purple)
64 Bill Black (Elvis Presley)
65 "Sweet" Charles Sherrell (James Brown, session man)
66 Phil Lynott (Thin Lizzy)
67 Billy Cox (Band of Gypsys)
68 Bruce Thomas (Elvis Costello & The Attractions)
69 Gary "Mani" Mounfield (Stone Roses)
70 Felix Pappalardi (Mountain)
71 Mike Rutherford (Genesis)
72 David Ellefson (Megadeth)
73 Matt Freeman (Rancid)
74 Ronnie Baker (MFSB)
75 John Alderete (Racer X, Mars Volta)
76 Robert Trujillo (Suicidal Tendencies)
77 Duff McKagen (Guns N' Roses)
78 Marshall Lytle (Bill Haley & The Comets)
79 Bill Gould (Faith No More)
80 Ray Pohlman (session man)
81 Me'Shell NdegéOcello (session woman, solo)
82 Doug Pinnick (King's X)
83 Tommy Cogbill (session man)
84 Glen Cornick (Jethro Tull)
85 Pino Palladino (session man)
86 Randy Coven (Steve Vai)

Continued on p.138

The 100 Greatest Rock Bass Guitarists. continued from p.137

66 *This instrument thing is out of hand. If Eric Clapton sold his guitar and bought a ten-dollar guitar, the kids would do the same.* 99

JEFF BECK

An advertisement for the "Frankenstrat"

Kramer
SOLID BODY ELECTRIC GUITARS AND BASSES

"It's very simply the best guitar you can buy today"
Edward Van Halen

THE FRANKENSTRAT

Eddie Van Halen rose to prominence playing a guitar he had made himself from a collection of guitar parts. The so-called Frankenstrat had an ash Stratocaster body and a maple neck, which he picked up for $130. He took the Gibson PAF humbucker from his ES-335. There was a single-coil pickup in the neck. But this was never wired with the humbucker as electrical wiring was not Eddie's strong point. Consequently, he also left the tone control out of the circuit.

As a bridge, Eddie used the Fender Tremolo System from his 1958 Stratocaster. A Floyd Rose was added later. The original pickboard was cut from a vinyl record and a strip of double-sided tape was used to hold spare picks.

He painted it black and white, but when other guitar makers followed suit, he came up with the famous yellow and black Charvel Hybrid version he called the "Bumblebee." Later he resprayed the black-and-white original with red Schwinn bicycle paint. The Bumblebee was buried with "Dimebag" Darrell Abbot of Damageplan in 2004. Fender have made 300 replicas of the original Frankenstrat, right down to the scratches.

CÓMPOSE YOURSELF

Eminent composers who
have written music for
the guitar include:

- ✪ William Walton
- ✪ Benjamin Britten
- ✪ Francis Polenc
- ✪ Pierre Boulez
- ✪ André Previn
- ✪ Malcolm Arnold
  (collaborated with Deep
  Purple on the first
  concerto for a rock
  group and orchestra)

Burns Bison

London guitar maker Jim Burns was known as "the
British Leo Fender." Burns' guitars were seen in the
hands of Hank Marvin, Jimmy Page, and even Elvis
Presley. The culmination of the career was the
massive Burns Bison, so called because when jazz
guitarist Ike Isaacs saw its curled horns, he said:
"It looks like a bl**dy bison." But the Bison was
too expensive for mass production and only 49
were made. Legend has it that number fifty was
turned into a coffee table.

TAYLOR T5

2005

From the mid 1970s Californian guitar maker Bob Taylor had been building his reputation as a maker of acoustic guitars. Then in the early 2000s he decided to go electric. The T5 is a slimline, hollow-body guitar with stylized f-holes and a pickup that looks like a Telecaster's neck single coil. In fact, it is a stacked humbucker. Instead of putting the two coils side by side, as in a Gibson guitar, they are mounted one on top of the other. There is an acoustic sensor under the top with another acoustic pickup in the neck block. A five-way pickup selector offers electric, acoustic, or combined tones. A custom version offers a choice of exotic woods with hardware in gold instead of chrome.

2005 Taylor T5

Ebony overlay on headsock

Rosewood fingerboard

Two soft-grip tone controls

Acoustic sensors in neck block and inside body

Volume control

Stacked humbucker pickup

Sapele mahogany body, routed out to give semi-solid construction

Stylized f-holes

Spruce or maple top (Hawaiian koa, cocobolo, or walnut on custom)

Jason Mraz at the Outside Lands Music and Arts Festival, 2009

Famous players

★ Dave Edmunds

★ Carina Ricco

★ Dave Matthews

★ Jason Mraz

QUALITY

Taylor.

GUITARS

The Taylor Guitars factory is located in El Cajon, California, and has more than 550 employees (2008).

An eight-string Brahms guitar made by the luthier Erez Perelman.

> **Keith Richards uses a Telecaster, but he takes the sixth string off and tunes it to G. That's what The Rolling Stones use all the time.**
>
> IKE TURNER

The more the merrier

Classical guitars sometimes have more than the standard six strings:

✪ **Seven Strings**: The French guitarist Napoleon Coste (1805–83) composed works for the seven-string guitar. Originally Portuguese, there are now Russian and Brazilian versions.

✪ **Eight Strings**: An eight-string guitar was originally built in 1994 to play Johannes Brahms' "Themes and Variation Opus 21a." Hence it is also known at the Brahms guitar. It is basically a six-string guitar with an extra lower and higher string added. The great Brazilian guitarist and composer Raphael Rabello has played it.

✪ **Nine Strings**: The Vox Mark IX and the Vox Phantom IX electric guitars.

✪ **Ten Strings**: A ten-string extended range guitar was built in 1963 by José Ramírez III (1922–95) for Spanish guitarist Narciso Yepes (1927–97). When Yepes first asked Ramírez to build it for him, Ramírez said it was impossible, but Yepes pointed out that there had been ten-string guitars in the 18th and 19th centuries.

✪ **Eleven Strings**: The Swedish luthier Georg Bolin made eleven-string guitars in the 1960s. They are used for playing lute music, particularly Bach. U.S. guitar maker Walter Stanul also makes an eleven-string instrument called the Archguitar.

✪ **Twelve Strings**: 12-string guitars come in both electric and acoustic versions.

✪ **Thirteen Strings**: Both Bolin and Stanul made thirteen-string versions.

✪ **Fourteen Strings**: In Mexico they double-string seven-course guitars.

✪ **Fifteen Strings**: "Fieldy" Arvizu from the nu-metal band Korn has a custom-built Ibanez K-15 triple five-string bass.

✪ **Twenty-five Strings**: The guitarrón chileno from Chile has five courses of five strings.

HOT FOR HOFNERS

The German guitar manufacturer Karl Höfner GmbH was founded in 1887 in Schönbach, which is now in the Czech Republic. After World War II they moved to Bubenreuth in West Germany and profited from the enthusiasm for jazz of the Allied troops stationed there, and introduced a range of arch-top guitars in 1951. Two years later, they went electric. U.S. bases were popular venues for British bands in the 1960s. Paul McCartney bought a Hofner 500/1 violin bass in 1961. It soon became the company's best-selling instrument. Keith Richards' first guitar was a Hofner, and The Rolling Stones' bassist Bill Wyman also had one.

A Hofner 500/1 violin bass

The future isn't plastic

In 1961 Italian accordion maker Oliviero Pigini & Company wanted to get into the booming market for electric guitars. The firm were used to molding plastic to make accordions, so gave their new Eko guitar line plastic bodies. Other Italian manufacturers such as Bartolini, Crucianelli, and Gemelli followed suit. By the end of the decade, the company saw the error of its ways and turned to more conventional construction materials.

A 1964 Eko 700 4V

A six-string Mosrite Strawberry Alarm Clock guitar from Ed Roman

Strawberry Alarm Clock

Mosrite made futuristic guitars suspended in an oval frame for the psychedelic rock band Strawberry Alarm Clock, best known for their 1967 hit "Incense and Peppermints." Ed King of Lynyrd Skynyrd was one of the original members of Strawberry Alarm Clock. The guitars are still available from Ed Roman in Las Vegas.

A 12-string Mosrite Strawberry Alarm Clock guitar from Ed Roman

TWO CHORDS GOOD

It's often said that a rock guitarist needs only to master three chords to play. But Lou Reed reckoned that two chords were enough—and proved it with the Velvet Underground.

TOP 10

CLASSICAL GUITARISTS

The following guitarists were chosen by visitors to the digitaldreamdoor.com website:

1 Andrés Segovia
2 Agustin Barrios Mangore
3 Julian Bream
4 John Williams
5 Narciso Yepes
6 Christopher Parkening
7 Alexandre Lagoya and Ida Presti
8 Manuel Barrueco
9 Kazuhito Yamashita
10 Pepe Romero

Stand-in Broonzy

An ex-preacher, Big Bill Broonzy came to fame filling in for Robert Johnson, who had just died, at a ground-breaking blues concert at Carnegie Hall in 1938. A sophisticated, urban musician in the Chicago mold, he reinvented himself as a coveralls-clad folk singer in the 1940s, playing a blond Gibson L-7 arch-top, and later a Martin 000-28.

Gibson ES-335

Lucille

B.B. King named all his guitars Lucille after he nearly died retrieving his beloved $30 guitar from a fire in a dance hall. The blaze had started during a fight between two men over a woman called Lucille. He named his guitar for her as a reminder never again to run into a burning building or fight over women. His most famous and distinctive Lucille was the Gibson ES-335 he bought in 1958.

NATIONAL AIRLINE MAP

1962

The National story is a complex one. The company made metal-bodied multi-cone resonator guitars. It was set up in the 1920s by Czechoslovakian-born John, Ed, and Rudy Dopyera. Later they split from the company and set up Dobro to build wooden-bodied, single-cone resonators. The two companies merged in 1934 to form the National-Dobro Corporation and in 1942 it became Valco, making Airline guitars for mail-order companies as well as the Supro and National brands. They then began making the "map" range, so called because of the unusual shape of the body that was said to resemble a map of the United States. It was made from Res-O-Glass, a type of fiberglass. Valco closed down in 1968, but Eastwood Guitars of Ontario, Canada, still make Airline Map guitars.

1963 National Newport 82

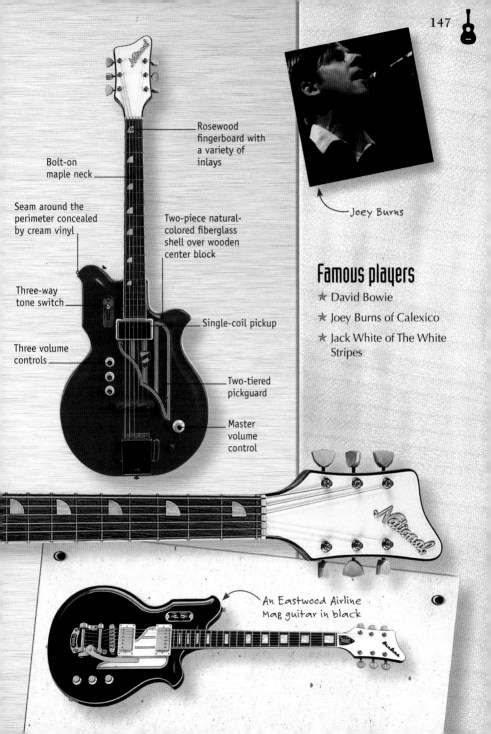

Rosewood fingerboard with a variety of inlays

Bolt-on maple neck

Seam around the perimeter concealed by cream vinyl

Two-piece natural-colored fiberglass shell over wooden center block

Three-way tone switch

Single-coil pickup

Three volume controls

Two-tiered pickguard

Master volume control

Joey Burns

Famous players

★ David Bowie

★ Joey Burns of Calexico

★ Jack White of The White Stripes

An Eastwood Airline Map guitar in black

Bigsby and Travis

In 1948 motorcycle designer Paul Bigsby (1899–1968) developed a solid-body electric guitar with country musician Merle Travis, which they named the Bigsby Travis. Two years earlier, Travis had asked Bigsby to repair a vibrato on a Gibson L-10. Instead of fixing the worn-out unit, Bigsby build a new one to his own design, and fitted it. This was the forerunner of the Bigsby vibrato tailpiece, also known as the tremolo arm, used by Gibson, Gretsch, and many other guitar manufacturing companies.

Classic Guitar Albums (1920–2000)

Listed by recording date.

1927–29 *Steppin' On The Blues*, Lonnie Johnson

1936–37 *The Complete Recordings*, Robert Johnson

1936–40 *Django Reinhardt*

1939–41 *Solo Flight*, Charlie Christian

1948– *Chess Box*, Muddy Waters

1950–54 *Complete Imperial Recordings*, T-Bone Walker, EMI

1954–64 *The Great Twenty-Eight*, Chuck Berry

1955– *In the Spotlight*, Bo Diddley

1957 *The "Chirping" Crickets*, Buddy Holly (UK)

1957–1960 *Best of Eddie Cochran*

1962–1966 *The Beatles*

1964 *Live At The Regal*, B.B. King

1965 *Bring It All Back Home*, Bob Dylan

1965–1970 *20 Essential Tracks From The Box Set*, The Byrds

1966 *Blues Breakers*, John Mayall's Bluesbreakers

1966–1976 *Decade*, Neil Young

Bigsby vibrato tailpiece on a 1955 Gibson ES-5 Switchmaster

1968 *Electric Ladyland,* The Jimi Hendrix Experience

1969 *Led Zeppelin II*

1970 *Fire and Water,* Free

1970 *Abraxas,* Santana

1971 *Sticky Fingers,* The Rolling Stones

1971 *Who's Next,* The Who

1972 *Machine Head,* Deep Purple

1974 *Feats Don't Fail Me Now,* Little Feat

1977 *Van Halen*

1978 *Dire Straits*

1979 *Regatta De Blanc,* The Police

1983–1984 *Hatful Of Hollow,* The Smiths

1987 *Appetite For Destruction,* Guns N' Roses

1987 *Sign O' The Times,* Prince

1988 *Daydream Nation,* Sonic Youth

1990 *Passion And Warfare,* Steve Vai

1990 *Family Style,* The Vaughan Brothers

1991 *Nevermind,* Nirvana

1993 *Watching The Dark,* Richard Thompson

> ❝ *Sounds are more important to me than trying to play a lot of notes... I practice scales, but then I go right back to trying to get certain sounds.* ❞
>
> B.B. KING

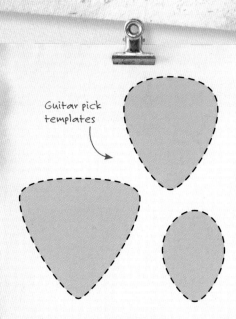

Guitar pick templates

Pick made from an old credit card

EMERGENCY PICKS

Here are three templates that you can use to fashion your own picks. Cut the templates out and then draw around them on the material of your choice to provide a cutting line. In an emergency, you could always grab your credit card—the perfect material and thickness—and get cutting.

TOP 20

ALBUMS OF THE MILLENNIUM

The guitar featured strongly in the pop music of the 20th century. In December 1999 *The Guitar Magazine* published a readers' poll, giving their "Album of the Millenium":

1 *Nevermind* Nirvana
2 *Dark Side Of The Moon* Pink Floyd
3 *Electric Ladyland* Jimi Hendrix
4 *Are You Experienced?* Jimi Hendrix
5 *Sgt Pepper's Lonely Hearts Club Band* The Beatles
6 *Led Zeppelin II* Led Zeppelin
7 *What's The Story* Oasis
8 *The White Album* The Beatles
9 *Texas Flood* Stevie Ray Vaughan
10 *Physical Graffiti* Led Zeppelin
11 *The Bends* Radiohead
12 *Abbey Road* The Beatles
13 *In Utero* Nirvana
14 *Ziggy Stardust* David Bowie
15 *Revolver* The Beatles
16 *Ok Computer* Radiohead
17 *Beggars Banquet* The Rolling Stones
18 *Automatic for the People* REM
19 *Highway to Hell* AC/DC
20 *Bring It On* Gomez

> 66 If we had five people on the stage, a 300-track studio, or a brand-new Les Paul, the creativity would be dead. 99
>
> JACK WHITE

GIBSON HARP-GUITAR

Gibson's 1992 harp-guitar, designed by Alex Gregory, was made by Roger Giffin, an English luthier who ran Gibson's Los Angeles Custom Shop for five years. It had 18 strings attached to a headstock that was over two feet (61 cm) wide. The outline resembles the solid-body guitars made by Gibson in the 1950s. It has an extended Seymour Duncan Zebra pickup, but no fretboard.

1916 Gibson U harp

Tapping

Instead of using the plectrum to pick a note, you can sound a string by tapping it against the fretboard. Using this technique, you can jump between high and low notes on the same string in a way that is otherwise impossible. This method was pioneered by Eddie Van Halen, who said: "Since you've got fingers on both hands, why not use both of them to fret notes?" The idea was picked up by Nuno Bettencourt, Randy Rhoades, and Joe Satriani.

Tapping on a six-string bass

Eddie Van Halen

Van Halen began playing homemade guitars through Marshall amplifiers. Since then he has used Kramers, Peaveys, Music Man, and Charvel through MXR phasers and flangers, and Peavey 5150 amplifiers.

LIPSTICK ON MY COLLAR

The pickups on Danelectro guitars were single-coil units mounted inside a chrome-plated tube. This led them to be called "lipsticks."

JACKSON SOLOIST

1984

In the early 1980s the Holy Grail for guitar makers was to combine the best of Gibson and Fender. So Wayne Charvel and Grover Jackson of Jackson Guitars, San Dimas, California, took the headstock and neck design of the Gibson Explorer, fitted a Gibson-style humbucker in the bridge, and added two Fender-like single coil pickups —or stack humbuckers that looked like single coils—to make what became the "Superstrat." However, they had, in fact, come up with something entirely new. This was the first "through neck" modern rock guitar. The neck and entire center section of the body were made from a single plank with pieces of alder or poplar glued on either side. Two models are available— Student or Custom. The Soloist can be heard on "Animal" by Def Leppard. Richie Sambora's Jackson was used on the album *Slippery When Wet*.

1990 Jackson
Custom Soloist

Explorer-style
headstock

Unbound
rosewood or
bound ebony
fingerboard

Maple
through neck

"Shark-fin" inlays
on Custom, dots
on Student model

Single-coil
pickups in
the neck
(some twin
humbucker
versions were
made)

Alder or
poplar wings

Humbucker
pickup in the
bridge

Floyd Rose or
Kahler vibratos

Famous players

★ Richie Sambora of
Bon Jovi

★ Phil Collen of
Def Leppard

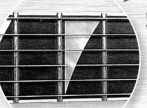

Pearloid
"sharkfin" inlays

Hawaiian
ukukele

NOTABLE UKULELE PLAYERS

* George Harrison
* Greg Hawkes, keyboard player of The Cars
* The Ukulele Orchestra of Great Britain, formed in London in 1985
* Hawaiian-born Jake Shimabukuro
* Israel Kamakawiwo'ole whose medley of "Over the Rainbow" and "What a Wonderful World" reached number twelve on Billboard's Hot Digital Tracks chart in 2004
* Indie performers Beirut Noah and the Whale, and Nevershoutnever
* Punk cabaret artist Amanda Palmer of the Dresden Dolls
* Singer-songwriter Sara Watkins of progressive bluegrass group Nickel Creek
* Singer-songwriter Jason Reeves on Colbie Caillat's debut album Coco
* Julia Nunes, who won the 2007 Bushman World Ukulele Video Contest

The Jumping Flea

The miniature Portuguese guitar called a cavaquino arrived in Hawaii with sailors from Madeira in 1879. The locals quickly renamed it the ukulele, which means "jumping flea" in Hawaiian. It is thought that this was because the fingers moving quickly up and down the fretboard resembled a jumping flea. The instrument reached a national audience after a ukulele and guitar ensemble named George E.K. Awai and his Royal Hawaiian Quartet played in the Hawaiian Pavilion at the 1915 Panama Pacific International Exposition held in San Francisco.

66 I like to get all the highs and lows, and with stereo you can run one amp set for treble and one for bass, and you can get the best of both. The Varitone is good for getting different tones, I leave my toggle switch in the middle and the Varitone at twelve o'clock; then I can get as much bass or as much treble as I want. 99

B.B. KING ON THE GIBSON ES-355

A collection of Mesa/Boogie Mark I amps, combos, and heads

A Dunlop Manufacturing fuzz box

FUZZY MEMORY

Keith Richards claims to have been the first guitarist with a fuzz box to have a chart hit— "I Can't Get No Satisfaction" in 1965.

THE WEST COAST SOUND

In the early 1970s West Coast sound engineers Randall Smith and Paul Rivera began beefing up Fender, Deluxe Reverb, and Princeton amplifiers. They used large transformers and high-powered output tubes. A gain control regulated the amount of natural distortion in the system, while a master volume control tapped into the distortion at different levels of "break up." Other firms followed suit. Even Fender hopped on the bandwagon. But the most famous name in the field was Mesa/Boogie. For a while, a Gibson ES-335 hooked up to a Mesa/Boogie Mark I or Mark II was the standard set-up among West Coast musicians.

> **I'm sure that guy Jimi Hendrix did help us sell a lot of Stratocasters. But I could never forgive him for destroying his guitar on stage.**

BILL CARSON OF FENDER

Tartar source

The Russian balalaika is of Tartar origin. It is a triangular instrument with three strings. There are six sizes.

- ✪ Piccolo
- ✪ Prima
- ✪ Sekunda
- ✪ Alto
- ✪ Bass
- ✪ Contrabass

The last is almost too big to carry.

TOP 10

COUNTRY GUITARISTS

The following ten country-style guitarists were listed on the website topten.com:

1. Chet Atkins
2. Merle Travis
3. Joe Maphis
4. Roy Clark
5. Speedy West
6. Albert Lee
7. Maybelle Carter
8. Buddy Emmons
9. Noel Boggs
10. Jerry Bryd

Slowhand

Eric Clapton earned his nickname "Slowhand" from his ability to play the guitar extremely fast.

Stevie Ray Vaughan

SRV used a 1963 Stratocaster with heavy gauge, .013–.058 strings, tuned down to E-flat. The signal ran through a Fuzz Face, Octavia, Ibanez TS808 Tube Screamer, then on to a combination of Fender Vitroverbs or Super Reverbs, Marshalls, and Howard Dumble amplifiers.

THE HORSESHOE PICKUP

The first pickup patent filed by George Beauchamp and his Ro-Pat-In company—later the Electro String Instrument Corporation—featured a cumbersome horseshoe magnet that extended both above and below the strings. This system was quickly copied by other guitar makers, such as Dobro, Vega, National, and Epiphone.

1949 Spanish SP Rickenbacker with a horseshoe pickup

HOFNER CLUB SERIES

1956

Hofner began making the tops and backs for violins and other stringed instruments in the 19th century. The company began making guitars after World War II and by the late 1950s, when the craze for electric guitars hit Europe, they were considered the best name around. Initially, there were three models. The single pickup Club 40 and double pickup Club 50 had plain wood bodies and rosewood fingerboards, while the more flashy Club 60 had back and sides made from flamed maple, an ebony fingerboard, and inlaid pearl position markers. The Club 60 headstock was overlaid with ebony and decorated with pearl and Hofner's vine-leaf motif. The Club 70 was introduced in the 1960s, but it was not a success.

1956 Hofner Club 40

Laminated maple, mahogany, and beech neck

Rosewood fingerboard

John Lennon in 1964

Laminated maple back and sides

One or two black Hofner single-coil pickups (later "toaster tops," then Hofner humbuckers)

Hollow body

Ebony bridge with fret saddles

Small oval control plate (later rectangular)

Nickel trapeze tailpiece

Two volume controls

HOFNER

Famous players

★ John Lennon

★ Paul McCartney

★ George Harrison

★ David Gilmour

★ Roy Wood of The Move

★ Justin Hayward of The Moody Blues

66 *I really wanted a Gibson Les Paul, but I couldn't afford one. I tried the Hofner Club 60 and liked it—Paul McCartney had one, too—so I had it sprayed black to look like a Les Paul. I couldn't afford to have it resprayed by a proper guitar restorer, so I had it done by a friend who was a car mechanic. But the volume was good, it was light, and it stayed in tune well.* 99

JOHN McNALLY

Paul Tutmarc
with his electric
eight-string,
double neck
eight-string, and
four-string bass

TUTMARC'S TALE

In 1931 in Seattle, Washington, former movie crooner and guitar teacher Paul H. Tutmarc (1896–1972) and auto mechanic Art Stimson developed a larger version of a telephone transducer to use as a guitar pickup. They attached an iron blade with copper wire coiled around it to a large horseshoe-shaped magnet and placed it inside Tutmarc's flat-top Spanish-style guitar, then plugged it into a converted radio and were surprised by the mellifluous tone it produced. However, they were told that the American Bell Telephone Company already had the transducer patent tied up and dropped the idea. Tutmarc then watched as Rickenbacker, National, and Dobro Manufacturing all produced their own electric guitars. It was all the more galling that one of Dobro's patent applications had listed as the assignor his one-time partner Art Stimson. Tutmarc then set up the Audiovox Manufacturing Company, which made electric lap steel guitars. He went on to produce the first solid-body electric bass in 1935. However, he had no national distribution and his bass never reached a mass market.

Fender Stratocaster
with a Synchronized
Tremolo bridge

The sound of The Shadows

The Fender Synchronized Tremolo bent the tone of all six strings upward and downward. Lead guitarist of The Shadows Hank Marvin—the first person to own a Stratocaster in the U.K.—pioneered the effect. In 2009, to celebrate the 50th anniversary of The Shadows, Marvin's original guitar, serial number 34346, was reproduced in detail by Fender's Custom Shop in Corona, California.

NEW YORK, NEW YORK

Segovia gave the first recital of the classical guitar in New York in 1928. Five years later a show called "Las Calles de Cádiz" introduced flamenco to the city.

Andrés Segovia
in 1925

> 66 For the guitar is the most unpredictable and least reliable musical instrument in existence— and also the sweetest, the warmest, the most delicate, whose melancholic voice awakes in our soul exquisite reveries. 99

ANDRÉS SEGOVIA

ELECTRONIC EFFECTS

Here are some of the gizmos used by guitarists to manipulate their sounds:

- **Clean boost or volume pedal:** Boosts the electrical signal to compensate for losses induced by other equipment. It is also used to boost the volume when a player changes from playing rhythm guitar to a lead solo.

- **Compressor:** Dampens the onset of the note, while boosting the sustain.

- **Tremolo:** Rapid variation of the volume of a note. This is produced electronically and the rate is controlled by a knob. The misleadingly named "tremolo bar" on a guitar provides vibrato, the rapid variation of pitch.

- **Distortion and overdrive units:** Add overtones to create a "warm" sound. The unit can also clip the sound waves to produce a "dirty" sound. Initially caused by the limitations of electronic tubes, this is now simulated by transistors or microchips. Distortion affects the sound at all volumes, while overdrive only cuts in as volume increases, leaving low volumes "clean."

- **Noise gate:** Cuts out electronic hum, hiss, and static. It can be turned to an extreme setting to produce an ethereal sound.

- **Fuzz box or fuzz pedal:** Clips the curved sound wave until it is almost square, giving a heavily distorted or "fuzzy" sound.

A guitar multi-effects device

- **Equalizer:** Uses electronic filters to alter the volume of specific frequency ranges.

- **Wah-wah pedal:** Operates a potentiometer to alter the frequency spectrum and create a "vowel" sound.

- **Reverb:** Simulates an echo chamber.

- **Chorus:** Creates a narrow vibrato spreading the sound as in a chorus.

- **Flanger:** Creates a "spaceship" or "jet plane" sound by adding a delayed version of the sound.

- **Pitch shifter:** Creates a ripple effect.

- **Harmonizer:** A pitch shifter that adds a note to the original to create a harmony.

- **Univibe:** A foot-operated phase shifter.

- **Harmonic exciter:** Adds overtones to the upper registers of the sound.

" *This Machine Kills Fascists* "

WRITTEN ON WOODY GUTHRIE'S GUITAR

A modern authentic reproduction gittern

THE ROCK 'N' ROLL LIFE —MEDIEVAL STYLE

No sooner had the guitar come to England than young men took to the road and the rock 'n' roll lifestyle. In 1561 John Feld, a servant in Norwich, did "absent himself from his master his service and went running about the country with a gittern," while in Newcastle in 1554, the Merchant Adventurers Company complained of the "lewd liberty" the instrument has instigated in its apprentices, whose misdemeanors included "dicing, carding and mumming, what tippling, dancing, and brazing of harlot... what use of gitterns at night—what wearing of beards."

> 66 I would never want to play any sort of guitar that a hundred people—not just the five or six best rock players—can do much better than I can. 99
>
> JOHN WILLIAMS

A 1934 Esteso flamenco guitar

The flamenco guitar

The flamenco guitar is made from cypress or maple to make it light, giving a crisp percussive sound, and rosewood is favored over the more durable ebony for the fretboard. Wooden pegs are preferred to tuning machines and the table carries a distinctive golpeador, a plate to protect it against the finger drumming and slapping that are an essential part of flamenco music.

LINE 6 VARIAX 600

2011

The Californian company Line 6 was founded in 1996. Its main business was originally the digital recreation of classic amplifier and speaker sounds. In 2003 they moved into guitar design with the Variax, which could reproduce the sound of classic Les Pauls, Gretsches, Rickenbackers, Telecasters, Stratocasters, Nationals, 12-strings, acoustics, and even a banjo and a sitar. The company says that it is 25 guitars in one. The Variax is modeled to look and play like an electric guitar, although no pickup is visible. The six piezoelectric transducers are hidden beneath the bridge saddle.

Line 6 also produces a four-string bass version and dedicated acoustic versions that emulate nylon- and steel-string guitars.

Line 6 Variax 600

Andy Taylor's solo album Thunder

Maple fingerboard

22 frets

Maple neck

Solid body made from mahogany, ash, basswood, or agathis

Fixed bridge (tremolo on 600 and 700 models)

Bridge saddle

LINE 6

Variax

Famous players

★ Andy Taylor of Duran Duran

★ Ed O'Brian of Radiohead

★ Babydaddy of The Scissor Sisters

" The Variax reinvents the way we will access all the classic tones from vintage electric and acoustic collectibles from one single guitar. "

STEVE HOWE

THE 100 GREATEST ROCK BASS LINES

1 "Another One Bites the Dust" (Queen)
2 "Roundabout" (Yes)
3 "Money" (Pink Floyd)
4 "Super Freak" (Rick James)
5 "Thank You Falettinme Be Mice Elf Agin" (Sly & Family Stone)
6 "Ain't No Mountain High Enough" (Marvin Gaye/Tammi Terrell)
7 "Dazed And Confused" (Led Zeppelin)
8 "Badge" (Cream)
9 "Higher Ground" (Red Hot Chili Peppers)
10 "Taxman" (The Beatles)
11 "Freewill" (Rush)
12 "Brick House" (The Commodores)
13 "Thela Hun Ginjeet" (King Crimson)
14 "NIB" (Black Sabbath)
15 "Good Times" (chic)
16 "Bernadette" (Four Tops)
17 "London Calling" (The Clash)
18 "Sunshine of Your Love" (Cream)
19 "Jeremy" (Pearl Jam)
20 "Ramble On" (Led Zeppelin)
21 "No More Tears" (Ozzy Osbourne)
22 "Boris the Spider" (The Who)
23 "The Lemon Song" (Led Zeppelin)
24 "The Boys Are Back In Town" (Thin Lizzy)
25 "Come As You Are" (Nirvana)
26 "Stand By Me" (Ben E King)
27 "Come Together" (The Beatles)
28 "White Rabbit" (Jefferson Airplane)
29 "Would?" (Alice In Chains)

Continued on p.167

THE AMERICAN GUITAR

Throughout the 19th century, guitar makers were moving to the United States where the guitar continued to evolve. By 1900, small guitars were available from mail-order houses—including Sears Roebuck—for just a few dollars.

66 I wasn't surprised at all when Hendrix died. You knew he was going to die by just listening to his music. It was all there, he had done it and he almost had to die to finalize it. 99

ROY BUCHANAN

> 66 **Nobody could play like Albert King. His tuning was a secret and Albert made me swear never to reveal it.** 99

GARY MOORE

See-thru guitar

In 1969 guitar-guru Dan Armstrong built range of guitars in clear, acrylic polymer (Plexiglass) for Ampeg. The transparent body had a long sustain, but was very heavy. Production of the Plexi Guitar ended in 1971 after a falling out between Armstrong and Ampeg.

Continued from p.166

30 "Sweet Emotion" (Aerosmith)
31 "Schism" (Tool)
32 "Lowrider" (War)
33 "Guns Of Brixton" (The Clash)
34 "Take The Power Back" (Rage Against The Machine)
35 "Longview" (Green Day)
36 "Heart of the Sunrise" (Yes)
37 "Young Lust" (Pink Floyd)
38 "The Joker" (Steve Miller Band)
39 "Pump It Up" (Elvis Costello)
40 "Should I Stay or Should I Go" (The Clash)
41 "Jerry Was a Racecar Driver" (Primus)
42 "Break On Through" (The Doors)
43 "Only In Dreams" (Weezer)
44 "Sober" (Tool)
45 "Coffee Shop" (Red Hot Chili Peppers)
46 "Whipping Post" (Allman Brothers Band)
47 "Summertime Blues" (Eddie Cochran)
48 "After Midnight" (J.J. Cale)
49 "Last Ride In" (Green Day)
50 "The Big Money" (Rush)
51 "Susie Q" (Creedence Clearwater Revival)
52 "My Name Is Mudd" (Primus)
53 "The Day I Tried To Live" (Soundgarden)
54 "Strange Brew" (Cream)
55 "Peace Frog" (The Doors)
56 "46 and 2" (Tool)
57 "Soul To Squeeze" (Red Hot Chili Peppers)
58 "Fire" (Jimi Hendrix)
59 "Dock of the Bay" (Otis Redding)
60 "Under Pressure" (Queen)

Continued on p.168

Continued on p.169

AFRI-CAN

In Africa guitars have been made with bodies made out of oil cans. These instruments are light—less than 6½ pounds (3 kg)—and use at most one-fifth of the wood in a conventional guitar. Some have no wood at all, featuring an aluminum neck. Volume and tone control knobs are made from bottle tops. Classic "Afri-cans" retain retain the oil companies' branding. Others feature the flags of the world or traditional handpainted designs from South Africa.

— Starplayer TV Outlaw

Back to the future

In the 1980s German guitar maker Duesenberg made its name with futuristic designs. Then in the mid-1990s it turned to retro models, even adding Art-Deco-style scratchplates and vinyl with a crocodile finish on the Starplayer TV Outlaw.

Solid materials

The following materials have been used for making the bodies of solid-body guitars:

- ❂ Mahogany
- ❂ Maple
- ❂ Ash
- ❂ Poplar
- ❂ Korina
- ❂ Acrylic
- ❂ Aluminum

Maple

Aluminum

Mahogany

Ash

Poplar

Acrylic

Continued from p.168

94 "Rain" (The Beatles)
95 "Otherside" (Red Hot Chili Peppers)
96 "I Don't Want To Go To Chelsea" (Elvis Costello)
97 "Orion" (Metallica)
98 "Another Brick In the Wall" (Pink Floyd)
99 "Weak and Powerless" (A Perfect Circle)
100 "Smoke on the Water" (Deep Purple)

Paul Tutmarc with his electric bass fiddle

66 *People have always pitied the poor bass-fiddler ... who has to lug his big bull-fiddle home through the dark streets after the theatre closes. But he doesn't have to do it any more. Because Paul Tutmarc, Seattle music teacher and KOMO radio artist, has invented an electric bull-fiddle. One you can carry under your arm... The first electric bass-viol is only four feet tall, instead of six. It could be made a lot smaller, but Tutmarc didn't want to be too revolutionary right off the bat. Bass-violinists are a conservative race, and have to be accustomed gradually to the idea, he says.* 99

THE SEATTLE POST-INTELLIGENCER, FEBRUARY 1935

YAMAHA PACIFICA SERIES

1989

The Japanese company Yamaha started making guitars in the 1960s. Then in 1989 a team of designers and players got together at the company's Guitar Development Center in North Hollywood, California to start a program that would culminate in the Pacifica. The early model USA1 looked to the Telecaster, while USA2 emulated the Stratocaster, with "Superstrat" features such as a Wilkinson vibrato, Sperzel locking tuners, two single-coil pickups and a bridge humbucker, and a compound radius fingerboard, flatter at the top to avoid choking off when bending the strings. The Pacifica 604 features a new pickup configuration: four single coils configured as two independent single-coil pickups and one double single-coil unit, which provides a range of tonal variations. The Pacifica series are among the most popular entry level guitars.

1989 Yamaha
Pacifica 604

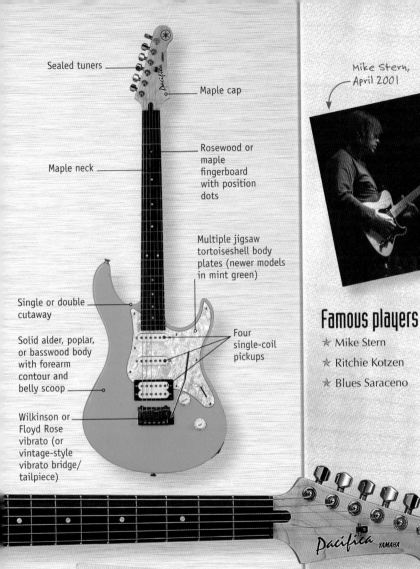

Sealed tuners

Maple cap

Maple neck

Rosewood or maple fingerboard with position dots

Multiple jigsaw tortoiseshell body plates (newer models in mint green)

Single or double cutaway

Solid alder, poplar, or basswood body with forearm contour and belly scoop

Four single-coil pickups

Wilkinson or Floyd Rose vibrato (or vintage-style vibrato bridge/ tailpiece)

Mike Stern, April 2001

Famous players

★ Mike Stern
★ Ritchie Kotzen
★ Blues Saraceno

Pacifica YAMAHA

WARMOTH NECK AND SPERZEL PEGS

The Pacifica 604 includes precision tuning machine heads from Sperzel, an American company, plus a neck made by the American manufacturer Warmoth.

Surprising people who played the lap steel guitar

★ Chuck Berry

★ Jerry Garcia (The Grateful Dead)

★ David Gilmour (Pink Floyd)

★ Steve Howe (Asia)

★ Brian Jones (The Rolling Stones)

★ John Paul Jones

★ Brij Bhushan Kabra (Indian classical musician)

★ John Lennon

Oahu lap
steel
guitar

Bill Haley
and his
Comets

ROCK 'N' ROLL

Bill Haley knew that he had to create a guitar sound to appeal to the new generation. He used a heavy four-to-the-bar beat and distinctive guitar breaks. When jazz guitarist Frank Beecher, who had played with Benny Goodman and Buddy Greco, came to audition, he was brought up short. "At the first recording session … I started playing with a jazz feel. I played the first four bars, and everything came to a halt. Haley said he'd never sell any records if I played like that. I had to stick to major scales."

TOP 10

FLAMENCO GUITARISTS

Votes from visitors to the website digitaldreamdoor.com resulted in the following ranking of flamenco guitarists:

1. Sabicas
2. Paco De Lucia
3. Ramon Montoya
4. Carlos Montoya
5. Paco Pena
6. Tomatito
7. Vincente Amigo
8. Nino Ricardo
9. Fahem
10. Tomas Michaud

Strat trem

Modern two-post tremolo

Floyd Rose-style locking tremolo

> 66 It was T-Bone Walker started off using electric guitar with the blues. Without T-Bone, that whole thing wouldn't have happened. 99
>
> BUDDY GUY

Tremolo arms

✪ The Bigsby Vibrato Tailpiece, introduced in the 1940s.

✪ The Fender Synchronized Tremolo or "strat trem," introduced on the Fender Stratocaster in 1954.

✪ The Fender Floating Tremolo or "jag trem," a "floating bridge," introduced on the Fender Jazzmaster in 1958.

✪ The Fender Dynamic Vibrato or "'stang trem," a "floating bridge," introduced on the Fender Mustang in 1964.

✪ The Floyd Rose locking tremolo, a version of the Fender Synchronized Tremolo, developed in the late 1970s.

✪ The Kahler Tremolo System, a cam-driven design used on pedal steel guitars from 1979.

✪ The Fender Two-point Synchronized Tremolo, a variant of the original Synchronized Tremolo, introduced in 1986.

✪ The Stetsbar tremolo, a cam-driven design used on pedal steel guitars, developed in the late 1980s.

Milton Brown and His Musical Brownies Selected Favorites Volume 4

FIRST ELECTRIC

The first recording on an electric guitar was made in January 1935 by "western swing" band Milton Brown and his Musical Brownies. Guitarist Bob Dunn converted his Martin for playing Hawaiian-style, and fitted it with metal strings and a pickup. The guitar was then used for a jazz-influenced solo break. Bob Wills and his Texas Playboys and Pee Wee King and his Golden West Cowboys soon followed suit.

JUAN BERMUDO'S FRETTING SOLUTION

According to Bermudo, the main problem with the vihuela de mano was the frets. They were made of gut and were wound around the neck, then tied at the back. The players had to tie the frets themselves, by eye and ear alone. Ten frets were usually thought sufficient, although eleven or twelve were sometimes used.

Bermudo came up with mathematical rules for positioning the frets. The simplest uses whole-number ratios to locate the second, fourth, fifth, seventh, ninth, and tenth frets. However, the vihuela de mano did not use the modern even-tempered scale but the ancient Pythagorean scale, which contained two semitones of different sizes. This presented problems where the frets spanned all the strings; some positions on some of the strings did not produce the right note. Bermudo suggested placing two frets close together, one behind the other, so that both semitones could be played. For this to work, the rear fret had to be thicker, so the string did not touch the one in front. Bermudo also concluded that it made more sense to make frets from steel or ivory instead of gut.

That's Rich

B.C. Rich have made a series of whacky shaped solid-body guitars. But they started out in a more conservative fashion. Bernardo Chavez Rico, a native of Los Angeles, built classical and flamenco guitars in the family business, Bernardo's Valencian Guitar Shop. In the mid-1960s he began to take an interest in steel-string guitars to capitalize on the folk-rock boom, He anglicized his name to B.C. Rich on the advice of a distributor. After repairing a electric guitar for Bo Diddley he got interested in electric guitars, making ten guitars inspired by the Gibson Les Paul and ten basses inspired by the Gibson EB-3.

He moved into making solid-body guitars and in 1971 came up with his first original design, the Seagull. Eric Clapton had one in 1975. This was followed by the Mockingbird and the Eagle in 1972 and the Bich in 1978. There followed a range of weird and wonderful guitars including the Warlock.

B.C. Rich's Warlock guitar

SET-UPS OF THE STARS

Keith Richards

In 1964 Richards was one of the first guitarists in the U.K. to have a Les Paul. However, he is more commonly associated with a Fender Telecaster, using a fuzz box and open tuning. More recently, he has favored the Gibson ES-345.

KRAMER BARETTA

1983

When Kramer Guitars approached Eddie Van Halen to make a signature model, he gave them his home-made "Frankenstrat" and told them to copy it in detail, right down to the year of the quarter lodged behind the tremolo. Kramer quickly realized that they could not mass-produce a replica for a reasonable price. Instead they came up with the Baretta with its distinctive "drooping banana" headstock. The original bodies were made by Sports in Connecticut, a sporting goods maker that made duck decoys and baseball bats. Although Van Halen had a great deal of input to the design, he never actually played one on stage.

Late 1980s Kramer Baretta with a custom paint job by Dennis Cline

Gotoh 90°
tab tuners

Rosewood
fingerboard

Oiled maple
neck

Schaller
Reverse Zebra
Golden 50
humbucker

Poplar or
maple body

Fender Jazz
bass-style
volume
control

Floyd Rose
locking vibrato

George Lynch,
October 2009

Famous players

★ Mick Marrs of Motley
Crue

★ George Lynch

★ Richie Sambora

KRAMER

KRAMER VERSUS KRAMER

In 1976 Dennis Berardi, Gary Kramer, and Peter J.
LaPlaca formed the B.K.L. Company to make
aluminum-necked guitars. By the end of the year,
Kramer had walked out, leaving the guitars that
bore his name to take the stage worldwide.

Tricks of the trade

In his heyday in the early years of the 20th century Charlie Patton (1887–1934) developed a wide range of gimmicks in his guitar playing performance, including playing the guitar behind his head, using a piece of brass pipe as a bottleneck, and playing "Hawaiian style" with a knife.

Gibson
0 style
guitar

66 **The whole secret behind the sound of The Rolling Stones is the way we work two guitars together.** 99

KEITH RICHARDS

GIBSON DESIGNATIONS

Gibson L model guitars have a round sound hole, while their 0 model guitars have an oval hole. Both were launched in 1902.

The 0 style A conventionally shaped, but very large instrument. By 1908 it had a mandolin-style scroll and a trapeze tailpiece. Costing a massive $150, it was discontinued in 1923.

The L style The L-1 was produced until 1926. The L-2 ran until 1908 and again between 1924 and 1926. The L-3 was produced between 1902 and 1933 and the larger 16-inch (41-cm) wide L-4 from 1912 to 1933.

Tunings

Spanish: E-A-D-G-B-E

Slack key: D-G-D-G-B-D. This has much in common with the standard G tuning on a banjo. It may have been introduced to the United States by an immigrant from Germany where this tuning was also used.

Open tuning: The strings are tuned to an open chord, the major or minor being achieved by sharpening or flattening the third string. This tuning was used by blues guitarists to make repetitive accompaniment easier.

Open E tuning: E-B-E-G-B-E.

Other tunings: D-A-D-G-B-D and D-G-D-G-C-D are also used.

Manzer bear-claw guitar head

MANZER'S BEAR

The Bear is an acoustic guitar that was designed and built by Manzer Guitars to celebrate their 25th anniversary. The name comes from its "bear-claw" top, a feature found naturally on some spruce trees, where the wood looks as if it has been gouged by the claws of a large bear. The inlay depicts the life of bears in their natural habitat. The bears shown are rare Kermode or so-called "spirit" bears. Although they are white like polar bears, they are in fact a type of black bear found only in northern British Columbia, Canada. On the guitar they are made out of mother-of-pearl.

IBANEZ AND VAI

Japanese guitar maker Ibanez began
producing guitars in the Fuji Gen-Gakki
factory in Matsumoto in 1962. Initially,
these were largely copies of other guitars.
Then in 1976 George Benson endorsed
their design of a hollow-bodied guitar
that resembled the Gibson ES175. After
a lawsuit the following year, Ibanez
decided to launch their own
designs and, in the 1980s,
commissioned guitarist
Steve Vai to come up with
some original ideas for
them. He is said to have
put his blood in the swirl
paint job on one of his
signature JEM guitars.

A floral pattern
Ibanez JEM 77

Endangered species

In 1990 the Canadian
Museum of Civilization
commissioned a customized
version of the Manzer Au
Natural. The fretboard carried
images of Canadian wildlife
that were on the endangered
species list, depicted in
mother-of-pearl, paint,
copper, bone, and abalone.
Featured species included
Dawson caribou, swift fox,
eastern cougar, ferruginous
falcon, whooping crane,
burrowing owl, sea otter,
and bowhead whale.

TO THE GRAVE

Bob Marley loved his
stripped-bodied Les Paul
Special so much that he had
it buried with him when he
died in 1981.

Andy Summers

The Police revolutionized the guitar sound of pop with Summers' use of an Electro-Harmonix Electric Mistress, a Memory Man, and a MXR Dynacomp compressor run through Marshall amplifiers.

ALL GREEK

In the 18th century everything Classical was much in vogue. So in 1780 the French luthier Pierre Charles Mareschal made a guitar that was shaped like a Greek lyre. It had two horns, one either side of the side of the neck, and was supposed to resemble a Classical kithara. It became a popular salon instrument, much in vogue because Queen Marie Antoinette played one.

Le Domino

In the 1930s the Chicago instrument maker Regal made a guitar named Le Domino. It had domino motifs on the belly, around the soundhole, and as position markers on the neck. It sounded like a Telecaster and was sought after by blues guitarists.

WASHBURN DIME SERIES

1986

"Dimebag" Darrell Abbott left Dean Guitars when his friend Dean Zelinsky sold the company. He moved to Washburn and the company based the design of the Dime series on the Dean ML—Abbott's first good guitar. Abbott was often pictured with the Dimebolt version of the Dime 333 with a lightning bolt graphic on the front. The Dime Culprit, featured here, was a highly popular model. It has 22 frets, a thin maple set neck, and a rosewood fingerboard. In the mid-1990s, Dean Zelinsky went back into production and Abbott left Washburn. Abbott was shot dead on stage in 2004. Dime models are no longer produced, but there is a thriving second-hand market.

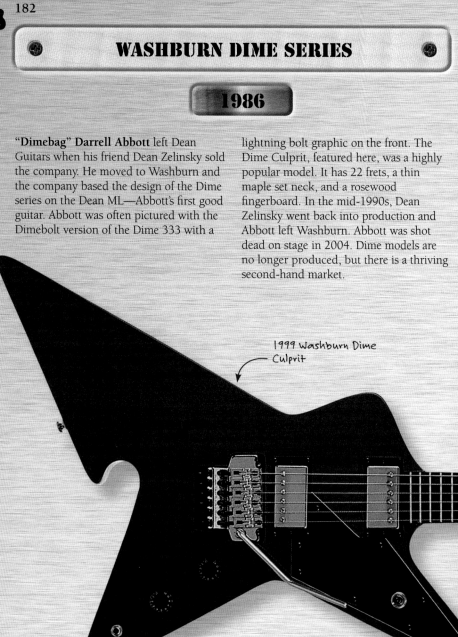

1999 Washburn Dime Culprit

22 frets

Maple neck

Solid alder body
with flamed
maple cap

Bridge with
dimebucker

Rosewood
fingerboard

Three-way
selector
switch

Two Seymour
Duncan
pickups

Floyd Rose
vibrato

Two volume
controls

Dimebag appearing
in an advert for
Dean guitars

Famous players

★ "Dimebag" Darrell
Abbott

66 I got home, picked up my ax, turned on the four-track
and just played it. I played three solos back to back on
Cemetery Gates. The next morning, the second and third
solos weren't bad, but the first had that first take magic!
I didn't touch it. 99

"DIMEBAG" DARRELL ABBOTT

Playing the U.S.A.

In 1982 Epiphone made a limited edition guitar with a solid mahogany body carved in the shape of the U.S.A. The U.S.A Map guitar has humbucker pickups, a stopbar tailpiece, a tune-o-matic bridge, and a maple neck with rosewood fretboard. It is a showpiece, but it is also a serious guitar. And you never need to get lost when you are on tour.

TOP 10

FOLK GUITARISTS

1 John Fahey
2 Davey Graham
3 Doc Watson
4 Bola Sete
5 Richard Thompson
6 John Renbourn
7 Bert Jansch
8 Sandy Bull
9 Robbie Basho
10 Martin Simpson

66 You could go out and eat and come back and the note would still be sounding. It didn't sound like a banjo or a mandolin, but like a guitar, an electric guitar. That was the sound I was after. 99

LES PAUL

DOUBLING UP

In 1966 Rickenbacker introduced the 336/12, which changed from a six-string guitar into a 12-string by means of a metal lever. It went out of production ten years later.

Jimi Hendrix on stage at the Royal Albert Hall, London, England, in 1969

Hendrix gets it covered

In England in 1966, musicians were experimenting with the sounds that you could get out of an electric guitar. Then Jimi Hendrix arrived in London. Eric Clapton was one of the first to hear him. "What we were stretching to do then, Pete [Townshend] in his way and I in mine, and then to walk into a club and see someone that you'd never seen before who'd got it covered… You see, we thought that we must be ahead of everyone else, so that if anyone's trying to do what we're doing they're nowhere as good as we are at doing it. And then to have Jimi lay all that down was quite heavy."

Index

Credits

Key: b bottom; c center; l left; r right; t top

2tl Outline Press Ltd 2b Outline Press Ltd 2tr Wikipedia 3c Manzer Guitars 8 tr Wikipedia 9t BC Rich 9cr National Museum of Music/The University of South Dakota/Bill Willroth, Sr., Photographer 9b Outline Press Ltd 10bl Weber Fine Acoustic Instruments/Dan Albright 11br www.GuitarPulp.com/Roger Gallimore 12cr C. F. Martin & Co., Inc. 13tr Steinberger 14b Outline Press Ltd 15b Outline Press Ltd 16tl Outline Press Ltd 16cr Wikipedia 18bl Nanotar 19c Wikipedia 20b Outline Press Ltd 21tc Outline Press Ltd 22c Starpics 23tl Hammacher Schlemmer 25l Antonio Dattis 25ct Antonio Dattis 24c Outline Press Ltd 24bl Getty Images/Hulton Archive 26b Outline Press Ltd 26tc Outline Press Ltd 29r Getty Images/ Michael Ochs Archives 30tl Outline Press Ltd 30br Vintage Nationals/Lenny Gerthoffer 31t Wikipedia 31br Washburn 32b Outline Press Ltd 33tc Outline Press Ltd 34b Getty Images/Richard E. Aaron 35 tl Getty Images/Chris Morphet/Redferns 36 c Bryan Adams 37 c Outline Press Ltd 38 c Wikipedia/Otto Erich 38 b Outline Press Ltd 39 tc Outline Press Ltd 39 tr Wikipedia/Mogwai73 41c Outline Press Ltd 42bl Outline Press Ltd 43tl Wikipedia 44b Outline Press Ltd 45tc Outline Press Ltd 46tr Getty Images/Michael Ochs Archives/Stringer 46cl Outline Press Ltd 47 l National Museum of Music/The University of South Dakota/Bill Willroth, Sr., Photographer 47cr National Museum of Music/The University of South Dakota/ Bill Willroth, Sr., Photographer 50b Outline Press Ltd 51tc Outline Press Ltd 52 l Outline Press Ltd 53tl Outline Press Ltd 55bc Outline Press Ltd 56b Outline Press Ltd 57tc Outline Press Ltd 57b Outline Press Ltd 58b Getty Images/Sergio Dionisio 59r Asier de Benito 59br Getty Images/Eric Schaal//Time Life Pictures 60tl Outline Press Ltd 60cr Outline Press Ltd 61tl Outline Press Ltd 62 b Outline Press Ltd 63 tc Outline Press Ltd 65 l Outline Press Ltd 66 t Outline Press Ltd 66 cr Museum of Making Music/Lynn Wheelwright 68b Outline Press Ltd 69tc Outline Press Ltd 69tr Wikipedia/Enrico Frang 71bl Epiphone guitars 72tr Chicago Music Exchange 72b Outline Press Ltd 73r Outline Press Ltd 74b Outline Press Ltd 75tc Outline Press Ltd 75tr Wikipedia/Leahtwosaints 76tr Getty Images/Theodore de Bry 77c Getty Images/ Redferns 78bl Dean Guitars 79r Outline Press Ltd 80b Parker Guitars 81tc Parker Guitars 82br Outline Press Ltd 83bl Outline Press Ltd 83cr Wikipedia 84l Outline Press Ltd 85tr Outline Press Ltd 86b Outline Press Ltd 87tc Outline Press Ltd 88r Outline Press Ltd 89t Outline Press Ltd 89 b Outline Press Ltd 90b Getty Images/Michael Ochs Archives 91br Mike Serrato 92b Outline Press Ltd 93tc Outline Press Ltd 94tl David Van Edwards 94r David Van Edwards 95bl Wikipedia 97bc Outline Press Ltd 98b Outline Press Ltd 99tc Outline Press Ltd 101tr Outline Press Ltd 102tr Wikipedia 103tr Getty Images/Michael Ochs Archives 104b Outline Press Ltd 105tc Outline Press Ltd 105tr Burns Guitars 106c Benedetto Guitars 107b Library of Congress/F. J. Brandholtz 108tl Wikipedia/Matt Myers 109t Getty Images/Buyenlarge 110b Outline Press Ltd 111tc Outline Press Ltd 112t Outline Press Ltd 114bl Getty Images/Michael Ochs Archives 115bl Guyton Guitars 116b Mike Serrato 117tc Mike Serrato 117bc Ed Roman Guitars 118t Manzer Guitars 119t Outline Press Ltd 120tr Outline Press Ltd 120bl Library of Congress/William P. Gottlieb/Ira and Leonore S. Gershwin Fund Collection 122b Outline Press Ltd 123tc Outline Press Ltd 124tr Outline Press Ltd 125tl Wikipedia/ Yuri Landman Hypercustom 125 bl Getty Images/Mansell/Time & Life Pictures 126 tc Getty Images/Keystone 126 l Ibanez Guitars 127 cr Wikipedia/Anitagraser 128 b Hamer Guitars/KMC Music 128 cr Outline Press Ltd 129 tc Hamer Guitars/ KMC Music 130 tl Wikipedia/Yuri Landman Hypercustom 131 tl Ed Roman Guitars 131 br Wikipedia/Leahtwosaints 133 tl Wikipedia 134 b Outline Press Ltd 135 tc Outline Press Ltd 135 tr Zemaitis guitars 136 tr pacopena.com 136 br Dream Guitars 137 bl Getty Images/March Of Time/Time Life Pictures 138 bl Outline Press Ltd 139 t Getty Images/Chris Ware/ Keystone 139 bl Outline Press Ltd 140 b Outline Press Ltd 141 tc Outline Press Ltd 141 tr Wikipedia/Moses 141 cb Taylor Guitars 142 tl Erez Perelman 143 tl The Paul Brett Guitar Collection/www. paulbrettguitarist.co.uk 143b Outline Press Ltd 144l Outline Press Ltd 144c Outline Press Ltd 145bl Outline Press Ltd 146b Outline Press Ltd 147tc Outline Press Ltd 147 b Eastwood Guitars 148l Outline Press Ltd 150br The Paul Brett Guitar Collection/www.paulbrettguitarist.co.uk 152b Outline Press Ltd 153tc Outline Press Ltd 155t Mesa Boogie 155cl Way Huge 157l Outline Press Ltd 158b Outline Press Ltd 159tc Outline Press Ltd 159tr Wikipedia/VARA 160t Greg Tutmarc 161br Getty Images/Hulton Archive 163t David Van Edwards 163br Outline Press Ltd 164b Line 6 165tc Line 6 167l Ampeg 168tr Alex Bond-Smith 168bc Duesenberg Guitars 169br Greg Tutmarc 170b Outline Press Ltd 171tc Outline Press Ltd 171tr Sven Petersen 172cl Getty Images/David Redfern/Redferns 172r The Paul Brett Guitar Collection/www. paulbrettguitarist.co.uk 173tr Outline Press Ltd 175r BC Rich Guitars 176b Mike Serrato 176tc Mike Serrato 177tr Glenn Francis/www.PacificProDigital.com 178l Outline Press Ltd 179br Manzer Guitars 180t Manzer Guitars 180bc Ibanez Guitars 181bl Outline Press Ltd 181tr Wikipedia 182b Outline Press Ltd 183tc Outline Press Ltd 183tr 184t Outline Press Ltd 185bl Getty Images/David Redfern 185tr Outline Press Ltd

iStock, Shutterstock

While every effort has been made to credit copyright holders, Quarto would like to apologize should there have been any omissions or errors, and would be pleased to make the appropriate correction in future editions.